Focus on GRAMMAR 3

FOURTH EDITION

Marjorie Fuchs

ALWAYS LEARNING

PEARSON

Focus on Grammar 3: An Integrated Skills Approach, Fourth Edition Workbook

Copyright © 2012, 2006, 2000, 1995 by Pearson Education, Inc.
All rights reserved.

Pearson Education, Inc., 10 Bank Street, White Plains, NY 10606

Staff credits: The people who made up the *Focus on Grammar 3, Fourth Edition, Workbook* team, representing editorial, production, design, and manufacturing, are: Aerin Csigay, Christine Edmonds, Nancy Flaggman, Ann France, Stacey Hunter, Lise Minovitz, and Robert Ruvo.

Cover image: Shutterstock.com
Text composition: ElectraGraphics, Inc.
Text font: New Aster

Photo credits: **Page 5** (left) Digital Vision/Getty Images, (right) Amos Morgan/Getty Images; **p. 13** (top) Bettmann/Corbis, (bottom) Bettmann/Corbis; **p. 14** Library of Congress; **p. 16** RIA Novosti/Alamy; **p. 22** Gerry Penny/epa/Corbis; **p. 49** (top) Shutterstock.com, (bottom) Shutterstock.com; **p. 60** Topham/The Image Works; **p. 68** RubberBall Productions; **p. 71** WENN.com/Newscom; **p. 72** Dreamstime.com; p. **83** Shutterstock.com; **p. 101** Shutterstock.com; **p. 102** Shutterstock.com; **p. 109** Images Source/Getty Images; **p. 120** Shutterstock.com; **p. 125** Colin Garratt/Milepost 92½/Corbis; **p. 128** Shutterstock.com; **p. 142** RubberBall Productions; **p. 147** (all) Shutterstock.com; **p. 166** Shutterstock.com

Illustrations: **Steve Attoe:** p. 2; **ElectraGraphics, Inc.:** pp. 4, 18, 34, 61, 87, 92–93, 97, 108, 131–132, 136, 153, 169, 171–172, 179; **Susan Scott:** pp. 25, 199, 190

ISBN 10: 0-13-216930-4
ISBN 13: 978-0-13-216930-1

Printed in the United States of America

7   16

CONTENTS

About the Author

Marjorie Fuchs has taught ESL at New York City Technical College and LaGuardia Community College of the City University of New York and EFL at the Sprach Studio Lingua Nova in Munich, Germany. She has a master's degree in Applied English Linguistics and a Certificate in TESOL from the University of Wisconsin—Madison. She has authored and co-authored many widely used books and multimedia materials, notably *Crossroads, Top Twenty ESL Word Games: Beginning Vocabulary Development, Families: Ten Card Games for Language Learners, Focus on Grammar 3: An Integrated Skills Approach, Focus on Grammar 4: An Integrated Skills Approach, Focus on Grammar 3 CD-ROM, Focus on Grammar 4 CD-ROM, Longman English Interactive 3* and *4, Grammar Express Basic, Grammar Express Basic CD-ROM, Grammar Express Intermediate, Future 1: English for Results,* and workbooks for *The Oxford Picture Dictionary High Beginning* and *Low Intermediate, Focus on Grammar 3* and *4,* and *Grammar Express Basic.*

Present Progressive and Simple Present

EXERCISE 1: Spelling

Write the correct forms of the verbs. Make spelling changes where necessary.

		-ing	*-s* or *-es*
1.	begin	*beginning*	*begins*
2.	come		
3.	do		
4.	get		
5.	go		
6.	have		
7.	live		
8.	look		
9.	meet		
10.	plan		
11.	play		
12.	read		
13.	run		
14.	say		
15.	start		
16.	study		
17.	take		
18.	watch		
19.	work		
20.	write		

EXERCISE 2: Present Progressive or Simple Present

Complete the paragraphs with the correct form of the verbs in parentheses. Choose between affirmative and negative. Use information from the cartoons. Use contractions when possible.

Amy

Dan

It's 6:10. Amy _____*has*_____ a 6:00 appointment with Dan at Café Blue. Dan
     1. (have)

_____ to the café. He _____ a watch, and he _____ like
  2. (walk)   **3. (wear)**   **4. (look)**

he is in a hurry.

    Amy _____ Dan, but she _____ his behavior. Why _____
       5. (like)   **6. (understand)**   **7. (be)**

he always late? She _____ at the café clock, and she _____ annoyed.
            8. (look)   **9. (get)**

    Amy _____ Dan's behavior _____ bad. But maybe it's just a
    10. (think)   **11. (be)**

cross-cultural misunderstanding. After all, Amy and Dan _____ from two different
                            12. (come)

countries, and people from different cultures often _____ in different ways.
                                13. (act)

EXERCISE 3: Present Progressive or Simple Present

Complete the postcards with the present progressive or simple present form of the verbs from the boxes. Use contractions when possible.

get	have	look	rain	stand	start	take	~~travel~~

A.

Dear Carlos,

I really love living abroad. We do a lot of traveling because the distance between countries isn't that big. Right now Ana and I ___are traveling___ through
                                              1.
England. At the moment, I _____ in front of Big Ben. It's a cloudy day. The
                           2.
sky _____ darker by the minute. It _____ like it's going to
        3.   **4.**
rain. (It _____ here a lot!) Ana _____ her camera, and
            5.   **6.**
she _____ pictures. I've got to run! It _____ to rain.
        7.   **8.**
See you in a few weeks!

Marcos

---

help	improve	live	love	mean	miss	speak	study	want

B.

Dear Amanda,

   Here I am in Paris! I _____ it here. It's a beautiful
                        1.
city. I _____ French and _____ with a French
        2.   **3.**
family—the Michauds. My French _____ because I always
                                 4.
_____ it "at home." I'm happy. This _____ fewer
    5.   **6.**
misunderstandings!

   The Michauds are great. They _____ me find a job. I
                                  7.
_____ to save enough money to travel in August. Why don't you
    8.
come and visit me? I _____ you!
                      9.
                        Melissa

EXERCISE 4: Affirmative Statements

Aldo and Emilia Bottero are students. Look at what they do every day. Complete the sentences about their activities. Choose between the present progressive and the simple present.

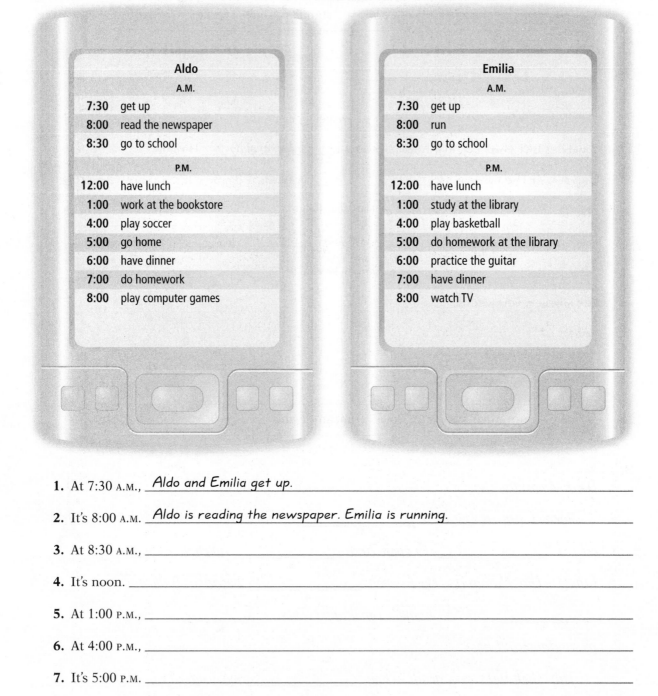

Aldo	
A.M.	
7:30	get up
8:00	read the newspaper
8:30	go to school
P.M.	
12:00	have lunch
1:00	work at the bookstore
4:00	play soccer
5:00	go home
6:00	have dinner
7:00	do homework
8:00	play computer games

Emilia	
A.M.	
7:30	get up
8:00	run
8:30	go to school
P.M.	
12:00	have lunch
1:00	study at the library
4:00	play basketball
5:00	do homework at the library
6:00	practice the guitar
7:00	have dinner
8:00	watch TV

1. At 7:30 A.M., *Aldo and Emilia get up.* _____

2. It's 8:00 A.M. *Aldo is reading the newspaper. Emilia is running.* _____

3. At 8:30 A.M., _____

4. It's noon. _____

5. At 1:00 P.M., _____

6. At 4:00 P.M., _____

7. It's 5:00 P.M. _____

8. At 6:00 P.M., _____

9. At 7:00 P.M., _____

10. It's 8:00 P.M. _____

Read the article about Aldo and Emilia from the school newsletter. There are five mistakes in facts about their schedules. Look at their schedules in Exercise 4. Then correct the mistakes.

Modern Language Institute Newsletter

Welcome, New Students!

We are happy to welcome two new students, Aldo and Emilia Bottero from Rome, Italy. The Botteros have a very busy schedule. They both get up at 8:30 every morning. Then Aldo watches TV, and Emilia goes for her morning run. They then leave for the Institute where they are studying English and American culture this summer. After three hours of class, they have

lunch together. After lunch, Emilia works at the bookstore. Both students love all types of sports. These days Aldo is playing soccer and Emilia is playing tennis. Emilia also plays the guitar. "Living abroad is a great experience, and we're very happy to be here," they said. "Our days are busy, but we always have dinner together. Just like back home in Italy."

1. They don't get up at 8:30.

    They get up at 7:30.

2. _____

    _____

3. _____

    _____

4. _____

    _____

5. _____

    _____

EXERCISE 6: Questions and Short Answers

Use the words in parentheses and the present progressive or simple present to write questions about Aldo and Emilia. Look at their schedules in Exercise 4 and answer the questions.

1. (Aldo and Emilia / go to school)

A: _Do Aldo and Emilia go to school?_

B: _Yes, they do._

2. (When / Aldo and Emilia / get up)

A: _____

B: _____

3. (Emilia / walk in the morning)

A: _____

B: _____

4. It's 12:00. (What / they / do now)

A: _____

B: _____

5. It's 1:00. (Aldo / do homework now)

A: _____

B: _____

6. (Emilia / do her homework at school)

A: _____

B: _____

7. (When / Emilia / play basketball)

A: _____

B: _____

8. (Aldo / play computer games before dinner)

A: _____

B: _____

EXERCISE 7: Adverbs and Word Order

Unscramble the words to make sentences. Use the correct form of the verbs in parentheses.

1. Aldo / the newspaper / (read) / always

   Aldo always reads the newspaper.
   _____

2. on time / usually / Emilia / (be)

   _____

3. never / school / Aldo and Emilia / (miss)

   _____

4. these days / they / (study) / English

   _____

5. usually / they / Italian / (speak)

   _____

6. (speak) / English / now / they

   _____

7. (do) / their homework / Aldo and Emilia / always

   _____

8. (be) / Aldo / tired / often

   _____

9. usually / (eat) / the students / in school / lunch

   _____

10. hungry / they / (be) / always

    _____

11. Emilia / at the moment / (have) / a snack

    _____

12. (go) / to bed / rarely / Emilia / late

    _____

Read the student's email. There are eleven mistakes in the use of the present progressive or simple present. The first mistake is already corrected. Find and correct ten more.

Hi, Andrew!

                I'm writing
How are you? ~~I write~~ you this email before my class.

I'm having a part-time job as a clerk in the mailroom of a small company. The pay isn't good, but I'm liking the people there. They're all friendly, and we are speaking Spanish all the time. I'm also taking classes at night school. I'm studying the language and culture of this country. The class is meeting three times a week. It just started last week, so I'm not knowing many of the other students yet. They seem nice, though.

I'm thinking that I'm beginning to get accustomed to living here. At first, I experienced some "culture shock." I understand that this is quite normal. But these days I meet more and more people because of my job and my class, so I'm feeling more connected to things. I'm also having fewer misunderstandings because of the language.

What do you do these days? Do you still look for a new job?

Please write when you can. I'm always liking to hear from you.

Brian

EXERCISE 9: Personal Writing

Write one or two paragraphs about your life these days. Are you busy? Are you relaxed? Use the present progressive and the simple present. Use some of the phrases from the box.

always	I sometimes
At the moment, I	Right now
Every morning	These days

EXAMPLE: My life is very busy these days. I'm working on an important project at my job. Every morning, I . . .

_____

_____

_____

_____

_____

_____

_____

_____

_____

_____

_____

Simple Past

EXERCISE 1: Spelling: Regular and Irregular Verbs

Write the simple past form of the verbs.

Base Form	Simple Past		Base Form	Simple Past
1. answer	*answered*		**16.** look	_____
2. begin	_____		**17.** meet	_____
3. buy	_____		**18.** move	_____
4. catch	_____		**19.** need	_____
5. come	_____		**20.** open	_____
6. die	_____		**21.** put	_____
7. do	_____		**22.** read	_____
8. feel	_____		**23.** say	_____
9. find	_____		**24.** see	_____
10. get	_____		**25.** take	_____
11. give	_____		**26.** think	_____
12. have	_____		**27.** understand	_____
13. hurry	_____		**28.** vote	_____
14. kiss	_____		**29.** win	_____
15. live	_____		**30.** write	_____

31. The past of *be* is _____ or _____.

EXERCISE 2: Affirmative and Negative Statements: *Be*

Look at the chart of famous writers of the past. Complete the sentences with **was, wasn't, were,** *and* **weren't**.

Isaak Babel	1894–1941	Russia	short-story writer, playwright[1]
Simone de Beauvoir	1908–1966	France	novelist,[2] essayist[3]
Karel Čapek	1890–1938	Czechoslovakia	novelist, essayist
Agatha Christie	1890–1976	England	mystery writer
Lorraine Hansberry	1930–1965	United States	playwright
Nazim Hikmet	1902–1963	Turkey	poet, playwright, novelist
Lucy M. Montgomery	1874–1942	Canada	poet, novelist
Pablo Neruda	1904–1973	Chile	poet
Wang Wei	699–759	China	poet, musician, painter

[1] **playwright:** a person who writes plays
[2] **novelist:** a person who writes novels (books that are fiction)
[3] **essayist:** a person who writes essays (short pieces of writing about a topic)

1. Simone de Beauvoir _____ *wasn't* _____ a French poet.

   She _____ *was* _____ a French novelist.

2. Wang Wei _____ born in 699.

3. Lucy M. Montgomery and Lorraine Hansberry _____ South American writers.

   They _____ North American writers.

4. Karel Čapek _____ a poet.

5. Pablo Neruda _____ from Chile.

6. Agatha Christie _____ American.

   She _____ British.

7. Isaak Babel _____ Russian.

   He _____ French.

8. Nazim Hikmet _____ from Russia.

   He _____ from Turkey.

9. Babel and Hikmet _____ both playwrights.

10. Pablo Neruda and Simone de Beauvoir _____ both born in the early 1900s.

EXERCISE 3: Questions and Answers with the Past of *Be*

*Use **was** and **wasn't** and the words in parentheses to write questions about the people in Exercise 2. Look at the chart in Exercise 2 and answer the questions.*

1. (Lorraine Hansberry / a playwright)

    A: _Was Lorraine Hansberry a playwright?_

    B: _Yes, she was._

2. (Where / Simone de Beauvoir from)

    A: _____

    B: _____

3. (What nationality / Pablo Neruda)

    A: _____

    B: _____

4. (Who / Wang Wei)

    A: _____

    B: _____

5. (Agatha Christie / French)

    A: _____

    B: _____

6. (What nationality / Lucy M. Montgomery)

    A: _____

    B: _____

7. (Nazim Hikmet / a poet)

    A: _____

    B: _____

8. (When / Karel Čapek / born)

    A: _____

    B: _____

9. (Who / Isaak Babel)

    A: _____

    B: _____

Complete the following short biographies with the simple past form of the verbs from the boxes.

~~be~~	begin	die	grow up	love	move	teach	use	write

A.

Béla Bartók (1881–1945) _____*was*_____ one of the most famous
1.

composers of the 20th century. Born in Hungary, he _____
2.

in a musical family. His mother _____ him how to play
3.

the piano, and at the age of nine, he _____ to write music.
4.

Bartók _____ the folk music of his native country. He
5.

_____ these folk tunes and folk music from other Eastern
6.

European countries in his own work. In addition to his compositions for musical instruments, he

also _____ an opera and a ballet. Bartók _____ to the United States in
7. **8.**

1940 and _____ there at the age of 64.
9.

be	begin	die	have	love	marry	paint	plan	study	teach

B.

Frida Kahlo (1907–1954) _____ one of the most famous
1.

Mexican painters. At first, she _____ to be a doctor, but after a
2.

serious accident she _____ painting from her bed. Her topics
3.

were her family and friends. She also _____ pictures of herself.
4.

Kahlo never _____ art in school. She _____
5. **6.**

herself how to paint. People _____ her work, and she had
7.

many admirers. In 1929, she _____ Diego Rivera, another very famous Mexican
8.

painter. Unfortunately, Kahlo _____ a lot of serious medical problems, and she
9.

_____ at the age of forty-seven.
10.

(continued on next page)

| be | build | fly | go | last | take place | watch |

C.

Orville Wright (1871–1948) and **Wilbur Wright** (1867–1912)

_____ American airplane inventors. The two brothers
  1.

_____ to high school, but they never graduated. They
  2.

_____ their first planes in their bicycle shop in Ohio. On
  3.

December 17, 1903, Orville _____ their plane, _Flyer 1_, for the first time. It was a short
                              4.

journey—just a distance of 120 feet. Wilbur, four other men, and a boy _____ from the
                                                                          5.

ground below. This first controlled, power-driven flight _____ near Kitty Hawk, North
                                                            6.

Carolina. It _____ only about 12 seconds.
              7.

EXERCISE 5: Questions and Answers

_Use the words in parentheses and the simple past to write questions about the people in
Exercise 4. Look at the information in Exercise 4 and answer the questions._

Biography A

1. (When / Béla Bartók / live)

   A: _When did Béla Bartók live?_

   B: _He lived from 1881 to 1945._

2. (Where / he / grow up)

   A: _____

   B: _____

3. (What / he / do)

   A: _____

   B: _____

4. (he / spend / his whole life in Hungary)

   A: _____

   B: _____

Biography B

5. (Frida Kahlo / plan to be a painter)

   A: _____

   B: _____

6. (When / she / begin painting)

   A: _____

   B: _____

7. (What / she / paint)

   A: _____

   B: _____

8. (When / she / die)

   A: _____

   B: _____

Biography C

9. (Where / the Wright brothers / build their first planes)

   A: _____

   B: _____

10. (both brothers / fly the *Flyer 1*)

    A: _____

    B: _____

11. (Where / the first controlled flight / take place)

    A: _____

    B: _____

12. (How long / the flight / last)

    A: _____

    B: _____

EXERCISE 6: Negative Statements

There were a lot of similarities between the Wright brothers, but there were also
differences. Complete the chart about the differences between Orville and Wilbur.

Orville	Wilbur
1. Orville talked a lot.	*Wilbur didn't talk a lot.*
2. *Orville didn't spend a lot of time alone.*	Wilbur spent a lot of time alone.
3. _____	Wilbur had serious health problems.
4. Orville grew a mustache.	_____
5. _____	Wilbur lost most of his hair.
6. Orville took courses in Latin.	_____
7. Orville liked to play jokes.	_____
8. Orville dressed very fashionably.	_____
9. Orville played the guitar.	_____
10. _____	Wilbur built the first glider.
11. _____	Wilbur made the first attempts to fly.
12. _____	Wilbur chose the location of Kitty Hawk.
13. Orville had a lot of patience.	_____
14. Orville lived a long life.	_____

EXERCISE 7: Editing

Read the student's short biography of a famous person. There are fourteen mistakes in the
use of the simple past. The first mistake is already corrected. Find and correct thirteen more.

                                                          was

Pablo Neruda (1904–1973) ~~were~~ a famous poet, political

activist, and ambassador.[1] He was born in Parral, Chile. His mother,

a school teacher, dies just two months after Neruda's birth. His

father work for the railroad. He no support Neruda's early interest

in writing. He wanted him to do something more "practical."

When he was seventeen, Neruda gone to Santiago to continue his education. At first,

[1] **ambassador:** a person who officially represents his or her country in a foreign country

he planned to become a teacher like his mother, but soon he beginned to write poems. He did not finished school, but he published his first book of poetry before he were twenty. In one of his love poems, he describe "restless rocks" at the bottom of the ocean. Like the rocks in his poem, Neruda did not stayed in one place. He spends decades traveling and writing poetry. His poems did show strong emotions and beautiful imagery.[2] In 1971, while he was Chile's ambassador to France, he winned the Nobel Prize in literature. Neruda dead two years later.

[2] *imagery:* the use of words to describe ideas or actions

EXERCISE 8: Personal Writing

Write a paragraph about your experience learning English. Answer the questions from the box.

> Where were you born?
>
> If you are now living in a different country, when did you come here?
>
> What language did you speak at home when you were a child?
>
> When did you begin to learn English?
>
> Where did you learn it?
>
> When did you start English classes here?

EXAMPLE: *I was born in Mexico, but I moved here with my family five years ago. When I was a child, I spoke . . .*

_____

_____

_____

_____

_____

_____

_____

_____

_____

_____

Frank Cotter is a financial manager. Read his schedule. Use the affirmative or negative past progressive to complete the sentences.

1. At 9:30, Mr. Cotter _____ *was meeting* _____

   with Ms. Jacobs.

2. At 9:30, he _____ financial

   reports.

3. At 11:30, he _____

   correspondence.

4. At 12:30, he and Mr. Webb _____

   lunch at Sol's Café.

5. They _____ at Frank's Diner.

6. At 3:30, he and Alan _____

   sales reports.

7. They _____ the budget.

8. At 4:30, he _____

   correspondence.

9. He _____ phone calls.

10. At 8:00, he _____ a lecture on

    the *Titanic*.

April 14 Wednesday	
9:00–10:00	meet with Ms. Jacobs
10:00–11:00	write financial reports
11:00–12:00	answer correspondence[1]
12:00–1:00	eat lunch with Mr. Webb at Sol's Café
2:00–4:00	discuss budget[2] with Alan
4:00–5:00	return phone calls
7:00–9:00	attend *Titanic* lecture at City University

[1] **correspondence:** letters and emails
[2] **budget:** a plan on how to spend money

Use the words in parentheses to write questions. Look at the schedule in Exercise 1 and write the answers. Use the past progressive.

1. (Mr. Cotter / meet / with Mr. Webb at 9:30)

A: _Was Mr. Cotter meeting with Mr. Webb at 9:30?_

B: _No, he wasn't._

2. (What / he / do at 9:30)

A: _____

B: _____

3. (Mr. Cotter / write police reports at 10:30)

A: _____

B: _____

4. (What kind of reports / he / write)

A: _____

B: _____

5. (What / he / do at 11:30)

A: _____

B: _____

6. (he / have lunch at 12:00)

A: _____

B: _____

7. (Who / eat lunch with him)

A: _____

B: _____

8. (Where / they / have lunch)

A: _____

B: _____

9. (Who / he / talk to at 3:30)

A: _____

B: _____

Read the newspaper article. Complete the story with the past progressive or simple past form of the verbs in parentheses.

HIT AND RUN

NEW YORK, June 30 Last Friday at 9:30 P.M., a blue Honda Accord _____*hit*_____
1. (hit)

thirty-five-year-old Lisa Coleman while she _____ the street at Broadway
2. (cross)

and 10th Avenue. Witnesses say that the car _____ and _____
3. (speed)   4. (not stop)

at the red light.

Frank Cotter, a financial manager at Smith Webber, _____ on his way
5. (be)

home from a lecture when he _____ the accident. "I _____
6. (see)   7. (walk)

along Broadway when I _____ this blue Honda. I _____ it
8. (see)   9. (notice)

because it _____ very fast. When it _____ the intersection,
10. (go)   11. (reach)

the driver _____ right through the red light. Seconds later, the blue Honda
12. (go)

_____ the pedestrian. I immediately _____ my cell phone
13. (hit)   14. (take out)

and _____ the police. The driver _____."
15. (call)   16. (not stop)

The accident _____ just a few blocks from General Hospital, and the
17. (happen)

ambulance _____ quickly. When it _____ to the scene of the
18. (come)   19. (get)

accident, Coleman _____ on the ground. She _____ from a
20. (lie)   21. (bleed)

head wound, but she _____ conscious and calm, and two police officers
22. (be)

_____ her about the accident.
23. (question)

Coleman _____ that she _____ the street when the car
24. (say)   25. (cross)

_____ through the light and _____ her down. "It all
26. (go)   27. (knock)

_____ so quickly," she said. "I _____ a green light, and I
28. (happen)   29. (have)

_____ the street when all of the sudden—boom! I _____ the car."
30. (cross)   31. (not see)

Coleman _____ her arm and _____ some injuries to her
32. (break)   33. (have)

head, but fortunately, they _____ very serious. Police are still looking for the
34. (not be)

driver of the Honda.

The police are interviewing another witness to the accident. Use the words in parentheses and the past progressive or simple past to write the interview questions.

1. (What / you / do / when the accident / happen)

   OFFICER: *What were you doing when the accident happened?*

   WITNESS: I was riding my bike home from school when I heard a loud noise.

2. (What / you / do / when you / hear the noise)

   OFFICER: _____

   WITNESS: I got off my bike and looked in the direction of the sound.

3. (What / you / see / when you / look in the direction of the sound)

   OFFICER: _____

   WITNESS: I saw a car—a blue Honda.

4. (Where / you / stand / when you / see the Honda)

   OFFICER: _____

   WITNESS: I was at the corner of Broadway and 10th.

5. (the driver / stop / when the accident / occur)

   OFFICER: _____

   WITNESS: No. The driver didn't stop. He immediately left the area. It was terrible.

6. (What / happen / next)

   OFFICER: _____

   WITNESS: I tried to get the license plate number, but the car was moving too fast.

7. (you / get a look at the driver / while he / drive away)

   OFFICER: _____

   WITNESS: No, I didn't. I don't even know if it was a man or a woman.

8. (What / the victim / do / when the car / hit her)

   OFFICER: _____

   WITNESS: I don't know. I didn't see her before the car hit her.

Read the newspaper article. There are six mistakes in the use of the past progressive and simple past. The first mistake is already corrected. Find and correct five more.

Last *Titanic* Survivor Dead at Age 97

LONDON, June 31, 2009 Millvina Dean, the last survivor of the 1912 *Titanic* disaster, ~~was dying~~ *died* yesterday in Southampton, England. She was 97.

Dean had no memories of the disaster. She was only two months old when she and her family were passengers on the luxury ship's first voyage. The ship sailed from Dean's hometown of Southampton, England, to New York City. On the night of April 14, they slept in their cabin when the ship hit a huge iceberg. Dean's father became alarmed and immediately sent his wife and two children to the lifeboats. Dean was believing her father's quick action saved their lives. Most people thought the ship was unsinkable. "My father didn't take a chance," she said.

Other passengers weren't as lucky. Just a few hours after the *Titanic* struck the iceberg, the ship was sinking to the bottom of the Atlantic. More than 1500 passengers and crew lost their lives, including Dean's father.

Dean's family returned to England, where she spent most of her long life. In her later years, she attended *Titanic* conferences and gave interviews. She moved into a nursing home when she was breaking her hip three years ago. Charles Haas, president of the Titanic International Society, said that with Dean's death, history lost "the last living link to the story" of the *Titanic*.

EXERCISE 6: Personal Writing

Write a paragraph about what you did yesterday evening. Use the simple past and the past progressive. Use some of the phrases from the box.

> While I _____ home yesterday, I . . .
>
> I _____ when I got home.
>
> While I _____ dinner, I . . .
>
> When I _____ dinner, I . . .
>
> I _____ English when . . .
>
> The phone _____ while I . . .

EXAMPLE: *While I was walking home from school yesterday, I stopped and got a slice of pizza. When I finished eating, I took out my cell phone and called . . .*

_____

_____

_____

_____

_____

_____

_____

_____

Used to and Would

EXERCISE 1: Affirmative Statements with *Used to*

Life in many countries isn't the way it used to be. Complete the sentences. Use **used to.**

1. In the past, _____ *people used to ride* _____ horses.

   Now people ride in cars.

2. In the past, _____ by candlelight.

   Now people read by electric light.

3. In the past, _____ over open fires.

   Now people cook in microwave ovens.

4. In the past, _____ all of their clothes by hand.

   Now people wash most of their clothes in washing machines.

5. In the past, _____ manual typewriters.

   Now people use computers.

6. In the past, _____ many weeks to get a message to

   another country.

   Now it takes just a few seconds.

EXERCISE 2: Affirmative and Negative Statements with *Used to*

Read the sentences about the assistant manager of a Florida bank, Mehmet Hassan.
Complete the sentences with the correct form of **used to** *and the verbs in parentheses.*

1. Mehmet _____ *used to be* _____ a full-time student. Now he has a job at a bank.
   (be)

2. He _____ stamps. Now he collects coins.
   (collect)

3. He _____ a car. Now he owns a 2009 Toyota Camry.
   (have)

4. Mehmet _____ the bus to work. Now he drives.
   (take)

5. The bus _____ crowded. These days it's hard to find a seat.
   (be)

6. Mehmet _____ in Chicago. Then he moved to Miami.
   (live)

7. He _____ Miami. Now he thinks it's a nice city.
   (like)

8. He _____ a lot of people in Miami. Now he has a lot of friends there.
   (know)

9. He _____ to Chicago several times a year. These days he doesn't go
   (return)

   there very often.

10. He _____ a lot of phone calls. Now he sends a lot of emails instead.
    (make)

EXERCISE 3: Questions and Answers with *Used to*

*Use **used to** and the words in parentheses to write questions about Lisa White. Look at the two ID cards to write the answers.*

1. (live in California)

   A: *Did she use to live in California?* _____

   B: *No, she didn't.* _____

2. Lisa recently moved to Los Angeles. (Where / live)

   A: _____

   B: _____

3. Lisa lives in a house. (live in a house)

   A: _____

   B: _____

4. This is her first job. (What / do)

   A: _____

   B: _____

(continued on next page)

5. (Which school / attend)

A: _____

B: _____

6. Lisa looks very different from before. She has short hair. (have long hair)

A: _____

B: _____

7. (wear glasses)

A: _____

B: _____

8. Lisa's last name is different from before. (be married)

A: _____

B: _____

EXERCISE 4: *Used to* or *Would*

*Complete the information about Lisa White with **used to** or **would** and the verbs in parentheses. Use **would** when possible.*

Lisa White's life has changed a lot in the past few years. She _____ used to be _____ a
                                                                      1. (be)
student at City College in New York. Her days were very long. She _____
                                                                      2. (get up)
early every morning and go to school. After class, she _____ to her part-
                                                              3. (go)
time job at a pizza restaurant. She _____ home until 8:00, and then she
                                         4. (not get)
_____ do her homework. Today, Lisa has a 9–5 job at a bank, and her
   5. (have to)
evenings and weekends are free.

Lisa is single now, but she _____ married. She got divorced last year
                                 6. (be)
before she moved to California. In New York, she and her husband lived in an apartment. Lisa

_____ the city by bus or subway. Now she has a small house and she drives
   7. (get around)
everywhere. It gives her a feeling of personal power. She _____ quite
                                                                8. (look)
different too. Today, Lisa has short hair, but as a student she always wore it long.

Lisa missed New York a lot when she first moved to L.A. She _____ back
                                                                  9. (fly)
whenever she had the chance. Now she is quite happy with her new life, although she still has a lot

of good memories of her old one.

EXERCISE 5: Editing

*Read the student's journal entry. There are eight mistakes in the use of **used to** and **would**. The first mistake is already corrected. Find and correct seven more.*

Sunday, Oct. 5

Today I ran into an old classmate. We used to ~~was~~ ^{be} in the same science class. In fact, we would often study together for tests. He was a very good student, and he always would gets A's. At first, I almost didn't recognize Jason! He looked so different. He would have very dark hair. Now he's almost all gray. He also used to being a little heavy. Now he's quite thin. And he was wearing a suit and tie! I couldn't believe it. He never use to dress that way. He only used to wore jeans! His personality seemed different too. He didn't use to talk very much. People didn't dislike him, but he wasn't very popular. In fact, I really would think he was a little weird. Now he seems very outgoing. I wonder what he thought of me! I'm sure I look and act different from the way I was used to too! I'm really glad we ran into each other. We shared a lot of the same memories. It was awesome! Maybe we'll see each other again!

EXERCISE 6: Personal Writing

Write one or two paragraphs about how your life used to be different from the way it is now.
Use some of the phrases from the box.

> When I was younger, I used to . . .
>
> Now I . . .
>
> I would . . . for hours.
>
> My friends would . . .
>
> Sometimes I would . . .
>
> These days I . . . ; but when I was younger, I always used to . . .

EXAMPLE: When I was younger, I used to have a lot more free time than I have these days.
I would spend hours with my friends. We would . . .

_____

_____

_____

_____

_____

_____

_____

_____

UNIT 5 *Wh-* Questions

EXERCISE 1: Questions About the Subject

Ask questions about the words in italics. Use **What, Whose, Who,** *or* **How many.**

1. *Something* happened last night.

   What happened last night?

2. *Someone's* phone rang at midnight.

   _____

3. *Someone* was calling for Michelle.

   _____

4. *Someone* was having a party.

   _____

5. *Some number of* people left the party.

   _____

6. *Something* surprised them.

   _____

7. *Someone's* friend called the police.

   _____

8. *Some number of* police arrived.

   _____

9. *Something* happened next.

   _____

10. *Someone* told the police about a theft.

    _____

(continued on next page)

11. *Someone's* jewelry disappeared.

_____

12. *Some number of* necklaces vanished.

_____

EXERCISE 2: Questions About the Object and *Why*, *When*, or *Where*

Use the cues to write questions about Megan Knight, an accountant in Texas. Then match the questions and answers.

Questions	Answers
e **1.** Where / she / live?	**a.** Two years.
Where does she live?	**b.** By bus.
_____ **2.** How many rooms / her apartment / have?	**c.** The first of the month.
_____ **3.** How much rent / she / pay?	**d.** Ling, Jackson, & Drew, Inc.
_____ **4.** When / she / pay the rent?	~~e.~~ In Texas.
_____ **5.** Who / she / live with?	**f.** Five and a half.
_____ **6.** What / she / do?	**g.** She's an accountant.
_____ **7.** Which company / she / work for?	**h.** Her sister.
_____ **8.** How long / she / plan to stay there?	**i.** Because she doesn't like to drive.
_____ **9.** How / she / get to work?	**j.** About $800 a month.
_____ **10.** Why / she / take the bus?	

EXERCISE 3: Questions About the Subject and Object and *Why*, *When*, or *Where*

Megan wrote a letter to her friend Janice. The letter got wet, and now Janice can't read some parts of it. What questions does Janice ask to get the missing information?

Dear Janice,

Hi! I just moved to _____ . I left Chicago because _____ .
             1.   **2.**

_____ moved with me, and we are sharing an apartment. I got a job in a _____ .
3.   **4.**

It started _____ . The town people seem nice. Our apartment is great. It has _____ rooms.
       5.   **6.**

_____ of the rooms come with carpeting, but two of them have beautiful wood floors. The rent
7.

isn't too high, either. We each pay $ _____ a month.
                          8.

We need to buy some _____ . _____ 's brother wants to visit her, so we really
                      9.   **10.**

need an extra bed.

By the way, _____ called last Sunday. I also spoke to _____ . They
             11.   **12.**

want to visit us in _____ . Would you like to come? Is that a good time for you? Just for
          13.

the record, I want you to know that there's plenty of room because _____ .
                                                14.

Write and let me know.

Love,
Megan

---

1.   *Where did you move?* _____

2. _____

3. _____

4. _____

5. _____

6. _____

7. _____

8. _____

9. _____

10. _____

11. _____

(continued on next page)

12. _____

13. _____

14. _____

EXERCISE 4: Editing

Megan is on a jury. She took notes and made a list of questions. Read her questions. There are eight mistakes in the use of **wh-** *questions. The first mistake is already corrected. Find and correct seven more.*

Questions

Why *did* the defendant ~~had~~ *have* $10,000 in his wallet?

Who gave him the money?

Why did the witness indicate Ms. Rivera?

Where did the defendant met Ms. Rivera?

Who keys did he have? Were they Ms. Rivera's?

Which bus did Ms. Rivera take?

Why she was in a hurry?

Whom saw her on the bus?

What time did she get home?

Why she did look so frightened?

Who she called when she got home?

What did happen next?

EXERCISE 5: Personal Writing

Imagine that a friend has just moved. Write your friend an email and ask questions about his or her new home. Use some of the **wh-** *question words from the box.*

How far	What	Where	Who
How many	When	Which	Why

EXAMPLE: Hi, Jason,

I just found out that you moved. How's your new home? I hope you like it. When did you move in? What does it look like? I know you wanted more space. How many . . .

_____

_____

_____

_____

_____

_____

_____

UNIT 6 Future

EXERCISE 1: Affirmative and Negative Statements with *Be going to*

Look at Professor and Mrs. Starr's boarding passes. Then read the sentences. All of them have incorrect information. Correct the information.

1. Professor Starr is going to go to Los Angeles.

    He isn't going to go to Los Angeles.

    He's going to go to San Francisco.

2. He's going to take the train.

3. He's going to travel alone.

_____

_____

4. The Starrs are going to leave from Chicago.

_____

_____

5. They're going to fly US Airways.

_____

_____

6. They're going to leave on July 11.

_____

_____

7. They're going to take Flight 149.

_____

_____

8. The plane is going to take off at 7:00 A.M.

_____

_____

9. The Starrs are going to sit apart.

_____

_____

10. Mrs. Starr is going to sit in Seat 15B.

_____

_____

Use the words in parentheses to write questions. Use **be going to.**

1. (What / you / do this summer)

   A: What are you going to do this summer? _____

   B: My wife and I are going to take a trip to San Francisco.

2. (How long / you / stay)

   A: _____

   B: Just for a week.

3. (you / stay at a hotel)

   A: _____

   B: Yes. We're staying at a hotel in North Beach.

4. (What / you / do in San Francisco)

   A: _____

   B: Oh, the usual, I suppose. Sightseeing and shopping.

5. (you / visit Fisherman's Wharf)

   A: _____

   B: Yes. We're going to take one of those city bus tours.

6. (your daughter / go with you)

   A: _____

   B: No, she's going to attend summer school. Our son isn't going either.

7. (What / he / do)

   A: _____

   B: He got a job at an Italian restaurant.

8. (When / you / leave)

   A: _____

   B: June 11.

   A: Have a good trip. San Francisco is an incredible city.

   B: Thanks.

EXERCISE 3: Affirmative and Negative Statements, Questions, and Short Answers with *Will*

Mrs. Starr is reading an interview about personal robots in the airplane magazine. Complete the interview with the verbs in parentheses and **will** *or* **won't**.

INTERVIEWER: We all know that robots are already working in factories. But tell us something about

the future. _____Will_____ people _____have_____ robots at home?
1. (have)

SCIENTIST: They already do! There are, for example, small robots that vacuum the floor. I believe

that before too long, personal robots _____ as common in the home as
2. (become)

personal computers are today.

INTERVIEWER: _____ they _____ the computer?
3. (replace)

SCIENTIST: No, they _____ the computer; but one day robots _____
4. (replace)

probably _____ computers.
5. (operate)

INTERVIEWER: That's amazing! What other things _____ personal robots

_____?
6. (do)

SCIENTIST: Well, for one thing, they _____ complete home entertainment centers.
7. (be)

They _____, they _____ . . .
8. (sing)   **9. (dance)**

INTERVIEWER: _____ they _____ jokes?
10. (tell)

SCIENTIST: Yes, they _____! But, as with humans, they _____ always
11.

_____ funny!
12. (be)

INTERVIEWER: What else _____ personal robots _____?
13. (do)

_____ they _____ more serious uses?
14. (have)

SCIENTIST: Yes, they _____. Robots _____ probably
15.

_____ care for this country's aging population. I don't believe they
16. (help)

_____ people, but they _____ some of the more routine
17. (replace)   **18. (perform)**

activities such as making the bed and loading the dishwasher.

INTERVIEWER: It all sounds great. Do you predict any problems?

SCIENTIST: Unfortunately, yes. Some people _____ happy with the spread of robots.
19. (be)

Not everyone's life _____. Some people _____ their jobs
20. (improve)   **21. (lose)**

to robots. And other people _____ criminal robots!
22. (create)

(continued on next page)

INTERVIEWER: _____ we _____ new laws to deal with robotic crime?
23. (need)

SCIENTIST: I'm afraid so.

INTERVIEWER: Tell me, how _____ these personal robots _____?
24. (look)

SCIENTIST: Well, they _____ exactly like humans, but they _____ us
25. (look)   26. (resemble)
quite a bit.

INTERVIEWER: And when _____ all this _____?
27. (happen)

SCIENTIST: Soon! I predict it _____ in the very near future. In fact, I'm sure you
28. (happen)
_____ some of it yourself!
29. (experience)

EXERCISE 4: Recognizing the Simple Present and Present Progressive When They Refer to the Future

Read this article about a new play. Underline the simple present and present progressive verbs only when they refer to the future.

CURTAIN CALL

A NEW PLAY

Next Wednesday <u>is</u> the first performance of *Robots* at Town Theater. Melissa Robins is playing the leading role. Robins, who lives in Italy and who is vacationing in Greece, is not available for an interview at this time. She is, however, appearing on Channel 8's *Theater Talk* sometime next month.

Although shows traditionally begin at 8:00 P.M., *Robots*, because of its length, starts half an hour earlier. Immediately following the opening-night performance, the company is having a reception in the theater lounge. *Robots* was a huge success in London, where all performances quickly sold out, but tickets are still available at Town Theater through March 28th. Call 555–6310 for more information.

Some people are flying to San Francisco. Read the conversations and circle the most appropriate future forms.

1. **A:** Do you know our arrival time?

   B: According to the schedule, we arrive / (we'll arrive) at 10:45.

2. **A:** Why did you bring your computer with you?

   B: I'll do / I'm going to do some work while we're away.

3. **A:** I'm thirsty. I think I'll ask / I'm asking for a soda.

   B: Good idea. There's the flight attendant.

4. **A:** Excuse me. Do you know what the weather is like in San Francisco?

   B: It's clear now, but it's raining / it's going to rain tomorrow.

5. **A:** Oh, good! They'll show / They're showing the new *Star Wars* on today's flight.

   B: Great! I missed it when it was playing in the theaters.

6. **A:** Just look at those dark clouds!

   B: I see. It looks like we're going to have / we'll have some rough weather ahead.

7. **A:** Be careful! Hold on to your cup! It's at the edge of your tray, and it looks like

   it'll spill / it's going to spill.

   B: I've got it. This sure is a bumpy flight!

   A: I know. I'll be / I'm glad to be back on the ground again.

8. **A:** I'm tired. I think I'll take / I'm taking a little nap. Wake me when the movie begins.

   B: OK. Sweet dreams.

9. **A:** It's 11:00 P.M. already!

   B: I know. We're going to arrive / We arrive late.

   A: Really? I'm surprised. We took off on time.

10. **A:** You know, I don't think the airport buses run after midnight.

    B: I'm afraid you're right. How are we going to get / are we getting to the hotel?

(continued on next page)

11. **A:** Hmmm. No buses. Well, that's no problem. <u>We'll take / We're going to take</u> a taxi.

 B: Do you think there <u>will still be / are still</u> taxis in front of the terminal so late?

 A: Oh, sure.

 B: That's good.

12. **A:** I missed the announcement. What did the captain say?

 B: He said, "Fasten your seat belts. <u>We're landing / We'll land</u> in about 10 minutes."

 A: Great.

13. **C:** How long <u>are you going to stay / will you stay</u> in San Francisco?

 A: Just a week.

 C: Well, enjoy yourselves, and thank you for flying FairAir.

14. **A:** Maybe <u>we'll see / we're seeing</u> you on the return flight!

 C: Maybe!

EXERCISE 6: Contrast of Future Forms

Complete the conversation with the correct future form of the verbs in parentheses. There will often be more than one correct answer. Use contractions when possible.

JASON: What _____*are*_____ we _____*doing*_____ tonight, Mom?
                                        1. (do)

MOM: We _____ a play after dinner. I got tickets before we left. Remember?
              2. (see)

DAD: What time _____ we _____ to be at the theater?
                                      3. (need)

MOM: The play _____ at 8:00, so I think we _____ there around 15
               4. (start)   **5. (get)**

 minutes before.

JASON: What about dinner? Where _____ we _____?
                                                  6. (eat)

MOM: We _____ dinner at a restaurant on Fisherman's Wharf. We have reservations
          7. (have)

 for 6:00.

JASON: How _____ we _____ there?
                            8. (get)

MOM: Well, according to this schedule, the hotel van _____ for downtown at 5:00.
                                                      9. (leave)

DAD: Hey, look at those clouds! It looks like it _____.
10. (rain)

MOM: No problem. We _____ our umbrellas.
11. (take)

DAD: You know, I'm tired. I think I _____ down for a while before dinner.
12. (lie)

MOM: Good idea. I _____ you in about a half hour.
13. (wake)

JASON: I'm really excited. This _____ a great vacation!
14. (be)

EXERCISE 7: Editing

Read this boy's postcard. There are five mistakes in the use of future forms. The first mistake is already corrected. Find and correct four more. There may be more than one way to correct the mistakes!

GREETINGS FROM
SAN FRANCISCO

Hi!

    I'm going
~~I going~~ to stay here for a week with my parents. Our hotel is incredible, and I spent the afternoon floating in the pool.

    We have a lot of fun things planned. Tomorrow night we'll see a play called *Robots*. Mom already bought the tickets for it. The play begins at 7:30, and before that we have dinner on Fisherman's Wharf. Right now we're sitting in Golden Gate Park, but we have to leave. The sky is getting very dark. It will rain!

    I call you soon.

               Jason

EXERCISE 8: Personal Writing

Imagine you are on vacation. Write a postcard to a friend. Tell your friend about your plans.
Use some of the words and phrases from the box.

for our next vacation	soon
in a few minutes	tomorrow
next week	tonight

EXAMPLE: Hi, Rosa,

I'm on vacation in Florida with my family. The weather is great, and we have a lot
of nice things planned. Tonight we're going to . . .

_____

_____

_____

_____

_____

_____

_____

_____

_____

_____

_____

EXERCISE 1: Simple Present or Future with *Will*

Complete the clauses with the correct form of the verbs in parentheses. Use the future or the simple present. Then match the time clauses to the main clauses.

Time Clause

_h_ **1.** When the alarm clock
_____rings_____ at 7:00 A.M.,
(ring)

_____ **2.** After she _____,
(get up)

_____ **3.** As soon as the coffee

_____ ready,
(be)

_____ **4.** While they _____
(eat)
breakfast,

_____ **5.** When they _____
(finish)
breakfast,

_____ **6.** After her husband _____
(wash)
the dinner dishes,

_____ **7.** As soon as they _____
(get in)
the car,

_____ **8.** Until he _____ his driver's
(get)
license,

_____ **9.** Until the rain _____,
(stop)

_____ **10.** By the time the day _____
(be)
over,

Main Clause

a. they _____ very
(be)
tired.

b. she _____.
(drive)

c. they _____ it.
(drink)

d. they _____ their
(fasten)
seat belts.

e. she _____ them.
(dry)

f. they _____ their
(need)
umbrellas.

g. they _____ the
(do)
dishes.

h. she _____'ll get up_____.
(get up)

i. she _____ a shower.
(take)

j. they _____ the
(read)
morning newspaper.

EXERCISE 2: Simple Present or Future (*Will / Be going to*) and Time Expressions

Vera is a student. Look at her future plans. (The events are in order.) Complete the sentences below with the correct form of the verbs in parentheses. Use Vera's plans to choose the correct time expression.

> ### Future Plans
> Take the TOEFL[1] exam
> Apply to college for next year
> Finish high school
> Visit Aunt Isabel
> Get a summer job and take a computer
>   programming course
> Fly to Brazil—Aug. 28
> Attend Sonia's wedding—Sept. 5
> Return to the United States
> Move into new apartment
> Look for a part-time job

[1] *TOEFL*®: Test of English as a Foreign Language

1. Vera ___will take___ the TOEFL exam ___before___ she ___applies___
               (take)   **(when / before)**   **(apply)**
   to college.

2. Vera _____ to college _____ she _____ school.
           (apply)   **(before / after)**   **(finish)**

3. _____ she _____ school, she _____ her aunt.
     (before / after)   **(finish)**   **(visit)**

4. _____ she _____ at a summer job, she _____
     (before / while)   **(work)**   **(take)**
   a course in computer programming.

5. She _____ her aunt Isabel _____ she _____ a job.
         (visit)   **(while / before)**   **(get)**

6. _____ she _____ the course, she _____ to Brazil.
     (before / when)   **(finish)**   **(fly)**

7. She _____ Sonia's wedding _____ she _____ in
         (attend)   **(when / before)**   **(be)**
   Brazil next September.

8. She _____ to the United States _____ she _____
         (return)   **(before / after)**   **(attend)**
   Sonia's wedding.

9. She _____ into a new apartment _____ she _____
(move)   (when / while)   (return)
to the United States.

10. _____ she _____ into her new apartment, Vera
(before / after)   (move)
_____ a part-time job.
(look for)

EXERCISE 3: Sentence Combining

*Combine these pairs of sentences. Use **will** or **be going to** and the simple present for the future. Remember to use commas when necessary.*

1. Vera will finish her summer job. Then she's going to fly to Brazil.

__*Vera is going to fly to Brazil*__ after __*she finishes her summer job.*__

2. Vera will save enough money from her job. Then she's going to buy a plane ticket.

As soon as _____

3. Vera's going to buy presents for her family. Then she's going to go home.

Before _____

4. Vera will arrive at the airport. Her father will be there to drive her home.

When _____

5. Vera and her father will get home. They'll immediately have dinner.

As soon as _____

6. They'll finish dinner. Then Vera will give her family the presents.

_____ after _____

7. Vera's brother will wash the dishes. Vera's sister will dry them.

_____ while _____

8. The whole family is going to stay up talking. Then the clock will strike midnight.

_____ until _____

9. They'll all feel very tired. Then they'll go to bed.

By the time _____

(continued on next page)

10. Vera's head will hit the pillow. She'll fall asleep immediately.

_____ as soon as _____

11. Vera will wake up the next morning. She's going to call her friends.

When _____

12. She'll have breakfast. Then she'll see her friends.

_____ as soon as _____

EXERCISE 4: Editing

Read Vera's journal entry. There are eight mistakes in the use of future time clauses. The first one is already corrected. Find and correct seven more. Remember to look at punctuation!

> I have a lot of goals, but I need to get more organized if I
> want to achieve them. So, tomorrow I'm going to start working on
> them. College is my number one goal. As soon as I ~~will~~ get up, I'm
> going to download some online college catalogs. After I examine
> them carefully, I choose a few schools that interest me and I try
> to set up some visits. Maybe I can even get some interviews with
> some teachers at the school. When I'm going to visit the schools,
> I'll also try to speak to other students. That's always a good way
> to find out about a place. After I'm seeing several schools, I
> decide which ones to apply to. When I get accepted I'll make the
> best choice. While I'm in school, I'll study hard and in four years
> I have my degree!

EXERCISE 5: Personal Writing

Write a paragraph about your goals. Use some of the phrases from the box.

After I . . . , I . . .	I won't . . . before I . . .
As soon as I . . . , I . . .	When I . . . , I . . .
Before I do that, I . . .	While I . . . , I . . .

EXAMPLE: *One of my goals is to save enough money to buy a used car. When I finish school, I'm going to look for a job. While I'm working, I'll . . .*

_____

_____

_____

_____

_____

_____

_____

_____

_____

_____

_____

_____

UNIT 8 Present Perfect: *Since* and *For*

EXERCISE 1: Spelling: Regular and Irregular Past Participles

Write the past participles.

Base Form	Simple Past	Past Participle
1. be	was/were	been
2. break	broke	_____
3. come	came	_____
4. fall	fell	_____
5. go	went	_____
6. have	had	_____
7. lose	lost	_____
8. play	played	_____
9. watch	watched	_____
10. win	won	_____

EXERCISE 2: *Since* or *For*

*Complete these sentences with **since** or **for**.*

1. I haven't known Ana ___for___ a long time.

2. She has been on my soccer team only _____ last September.

3. We've become good friends _____ then.

4. Our team hasn't been in a game _____ a few weeks.

5. _____ our last game, we've practiced a lot.

6. _____ weeks we've gone to the field every day after class.

7. We haven't lost a game _____ several months.

8. I have loved sports _____ I was a little girl.

*Complete the information about two athletes who have been famous since they were children. Use the present perfect form of the verbs in parentheses and choose between **since** and **for**.*

Michelle Wie (1989–)

Michelle Wie ___has been___ a golfer _____
1. (be)   2. (since / for)

most of her life. She began swinging a club at the early age of four.

Soon she was hitting the ball more than 100 yards, amazing her

family and neighbors. Maybe it was because of her strength that

Wie, as a child, announced that she wanted to compete against

men one day. Not only was she powerful, she was tall too. At the

age of thirteen, she was already 5'6". _____ then she
                                          3. (since / for)

_____ the height of 6 feet.
4. (reach)

When Wie was ten, she became the youngest player to qualify for the USGA[1] amateur

championship. That was just the beginning of her record-breaking career. _____ that
                                                                            5. (since / for)

time, she _____ to become the youngest golfer to participate in and win many events.
          6. (go on)

And, true to her childhood dream, she _____ in several all-men competitions.
                                        7. (play)

Wie turned pro when she was sixteen and immediately signed endorsement contracts[2] with

companies such as Nike and Sony. _____ then, she _____ to win many
                                   8. (since / for)   9. (continue)

tournaments and _____ tens of millions of dollars a year. _____ several
                 10. (earn)   11. (since / for)

years, Wie _____ a member of the Ladies Professional Golf Association, but she still
           12. (be)

hopes to compete against men and even beat them one day.

[1] ***USGA:*** United States Golf Association

[2] ***endorsement contract:*** agreement to do advertisements and TV commercials for a company

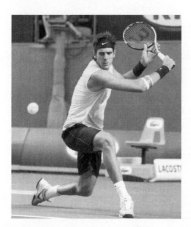

Juan Martin del Potro (1988–)

Born in Tandil, Argentina, Juan Martin del Potro, known as "Delpo,"

_____ a tennis player _____ he was
13. (be)   14. (since / for)

seven. He won his first senior match at the age of fifteen, and he

_____ to win many competitions _____
15. (continue)   16. (since / for)

that time.

Del Potro turned pro in 2005. _____ 2006, he
                               17. (since / for)

_____ many records—frequently finishing the year as
18. (break)

(continued on next page)

the youngest player in the top 100. In 2008, he won four titles in a row, and in 2009, he finished in

the top ten. He _____ also _____ millions of dollars in prize money
                                          19. (win)

_____ he turned pro.
20. (since / for)

The road to success has not been easy. _____ many years, del Potro
                                           21. (since / for)

_____ a lot of physical problems and he _____ playing many times
22. (have)   **23. (stop)**

because of injuries. But he always comes back. His long-time dream was to win the U.S. Open. In

2009, his dream came true. Not only did he win, but he beat Roger Federer, the number one tennis

player in the world at the time.

"_____ I was young," said the twenty-year-old 6'6" star, "I _____ of
24. (since / for)   **25. (dream)**

winning this trophy . . . It's an unbelievable moment . . . Everything is perfect." Many people predict

that del Potro will continue to have many more unbelievable moments in his career.

EXERCISE 4: Questions and Answers

Use the words in parentheses to write questions about the athletes in Exercise 3. Look at the information again and answer the questions.

1. (How long / Michelle Wie / be a golfer)

   A: _How long has Michelle Wie been a golfer?_____

   B: _She has been a golfer since she was four years old OR for most of her life._____

2. (How long / she / have a record-breaking career)

   A: _____

   B: _____

3. (How long / she / be a professional golfer)

   A: _____

   B: _____

4. (she / have any endorsement contracts)

   A: _____

   B: _____

5. (How long / Juan Martin del Potro / be a tennis player)

   A: _____

   B: _____

6. (How much money / he / win since he turned pro)

A: _____

B: _____

7. (What kind of problems / he / have for years)

A: _____

B: _____

8. (he / win any titles since 2008)

A: _____

B: _____

EXERCISE 5: Affirmative and Negative Statements

Read each pair of sentences. Use the correct present perfect form to complete or write a summary sentence that has a meaning similar to the two sentences.

1. a. Jack and Victor became golfers in 2004.

   b. They are still golfers.

   SUMMARY: _Jack and Victor have been golfers_____ since 2004.

2. a. Fei-Mei and Natasha competed in 1997.

   b. That was the last time they competed.

   SUMMARY: _Fei-Mei and Natasha haven't competed since 1997._____

3. a. Min Ho won two awards in 2008.

   b. He won one other award in 2009.

   SUMMARY: _____ since 2008.

4. a. Marilyn entered a competition in 2009.

   b. She entered one more competition last year.

   SUMMARY: _____ since 2009.

5. a. Victor and Marilyn saw each other in 2010.

   b. That was the last time they saw each other.

   SUMMARY: _____

(continued on next page)

6. a. Karl became a tennis player in 2009.

   b. He is still a tennis player.

   SUMMARY: _____

7. a. Karl lost two tournaments in February of this year.

   b. He lost another tournament last week.

   SUMMARY: _____ since February of this year.

8. a. Andreas went to a tennis match two years ago.

   b. That was the last match he went to.

   SUMMARY: _____ for two years.

EXERCISE 6: Editing

Read these online tweets[1] about sports. There are eight mistakes in the use of the present perfect with **since** *and* **for**. *The first is already corrected. Find and correct seven more.*

>   *for*
> What a great game! Marissa has been my favorite ~~since~~ years!
>
> I heard that Taylor got $350,000 for winning yesterday's tournament. How much money does he make since he turned pro? Does anyone know?
>
> Do you think Lee can support himself playing golf? He hasn't win a major tournament for two years. That's a long time!
>
> Karla didn't win a game since last year. I really feel bad for her.
>
> Walter has stopped playing twice since January because of injuries. That's really too bad.
>
> I haven't had the opportunity to attend a competition since three years. This one is awesome!
>
> I used to think golf was boring. Not anymore. I don't enjoy a sports event so much for years!
>
> I think Juan's game has improve dramatically since he won the last tournament.
>
> Antonio's positive attitude have helped him improve his game since he lost the match last month. I consider him a role model.

[1] **tweet:** a very short online message

EXERCISE 7: Personal Writing

Write about someone you know who plays sports. (You can also write about yourself.) Use some of the phrases from the box.

for a long time	since he/she
for . . . years	since then . . .
since 2010	since . . . not . . .

EXAMPLE: My friend Karl has been on the school basketball team for two years. His team has won many games since . . .

_____

_____

_____

_____

_____

_____

_____

_____

_____

_____

_____

_____

Present Perfect: *Already*, *Yet*, and *Still*

EXERCISE 1: Spelling: Regular and Irregular Past Participles

Write the past participles.

Base Form	Simple Past	Past Participle
1. act	acted	*acted*
2. become	became	
3. choose	chose	
4. clean	cleaned	
5. dance	danced	
6. drink	drank	
7. fight	fought	
8. find	found	
9. get	got	
10. give	gave	
11. hold	held	
12. keep	kept	
13. know	knew	
14. look	looked	
15. plan	planned	
16. sing	sang	
17. smile	smiled	
18. throw	threw	

*Complete the conversation with the correct form of the verbs in parentheses and an adverb—**already, yet,** or **still**. Use contractions if possible.*

TED: I hear you're looking for a new apartment. _____*Have*_____ you
                                     1.

   _____*found*_____ one _____*yet*_____?
      2. (find)   **3. (*already / yet / still*)**

MIA: No, and we're getting discouraged. We _____
                                                4.

   _____ _____ at more than 10, and we
     5. (*already / yet / still*)   **6. (look)**

   _____ _____ one that we like!
     7. (*already / yet / still*)   **8. (not find)**

TED: Well, don't give up. I _____ _____
                             9.   **10. (*already / yet / still*)**

   _____ at least 20. Are you working with a real estate agent? It may be
     11. (see)

   time to get some professional help.

MIA: No. We wanted to try to find something ourselves, so we _____ to an
                                       12. (not go)

   agent _____. But I think you're right. We may be more successful with
     13. (*already / yet / still*)

   an agent. Unfortunately, we _____ _____
                            14.   **15. (*already / yet / still*)**

   _____ a lot of time looking at apartments that were completely wrong
     16. (waste)

   for us.

TED: I know what you mean. _____ you _____ on
                       17.   **18. (decide)**

   a specific neighborhood _____?
     19. (*already / yet / still*)

MIA: No. We _____ our minds _____. What about
     20. (not make up)   **21. (*already / yet / still*)**

   you? Where do you want to be?

TED: We'd really like to stay in this neighborhood. We just need a bigger place.

MIA: Well, good luck!

TED: Thanks. You too.

EXERCISE 3: Questions and Answers with *Already, Yet,* and *Still*

Mia is going to move. She is very organized. Read her list of things to do. She has checked (✓) all the things she's already done. Write questions and answers about the words in parentheses.

Moving Checklist

- ☑ choose a moving company
- ☐ find a professional painter
- ☑ collect boxes for packing
- ☑ get a change-of-address form from the post office
- ☐ begin to pack clothes
- ☑ make a list of cleaning supplies
- ☐ clean the refrigerator and stove
- ☑ buy two bookcases
- ☑ give away the old couch
- ☐ buy a new couch
- ☐ throw away old magazines
- ☐ invite the neighbors over for a good-bye party

1. **A:** (moving company) *Has she chosen a moving company yet?*

   B: *Yes, she's already chosen a moving company.*

2. **A:** (clothes) *Has she begun to pack clothes yet?*

   B: *No, she hasn't begun to pack clothes yet.* OR *She still hasn't begun to pack clothes.*

3. **A:** (bookcases) _____

   B: _____

4. **A:** (magazines) _____

   B: _____

5. **A:** (painter) _____

   B: _____

6. **A:** (boxes) _____

   B: _____

7. A: (new couch) _____

    B: _____

8. A: (old couch) _____

    B: _____

9. A: (refrigerator and stove) _____

    B: _____

10. A: (cleaning supplies) _____

    B: _____

11. A: (change-of-address form) _____

    B: _____

12. A: (the neighbors) _____

    B: _____

EXERCISE 4: Editing

Mia sent an email to her friend. There are seven mistakes in the use of the present perfect with **already, yet,** *and* **still.** *The first one is already corrected. Find and correct six more.*

Hi! I'm writing to you from our new apartment! It took us a long time to find, but finally,

with some professional advice, we were successful. We've already ~~be~~ *been* here two weeks,

and we feel very much at home. But there's still a lot to do. Believe it or not, we haven't

unpacked all the boxes still! We took most of our old furniture, so we don't need to get too

much new stuff. We had to buy a new couch for the living room, but they haven't

delivered it already.

We've already meet some of our new neighbors. They seem very nice. One of them have

already invited us over for coffee.

Had you made vacation plans yet? As soon as we get the couch (it's a sleeper), we'd

love for you to visit. Already we've planned places to take you when you come, but let us

know if there are any specific things you'd like to do or see. —Mia

EXERCISE 5: Personal Writing

A. *Make a "To Do" list of things you need to do in the next few days or weeks. Include some things you have already done, and check (✓) those things.*

	To Do
☐	
☐	
☐	
☐	
☐	
☐	
☐	
☐	

B. *Write an email to a friend. Tell him or her about what you* **have already done,** *what you* **haven't done yet,** *and what you* **still haven't done.**

EXAMPLE: *My cousins are coming to visit this weekend, and I have a lot of things to do before they get here. I've already cleaned the apartment, but I haven't gone shopping for food yet. And I know they'll want to see a play, but I still haven't gotten tickets . . .*

_____

_____

_____

_____

_____

_____

_____

_____

_____

Present Perfect: Indefinite Past

EXERCISE 1: Spelling: Regular and Irregular Past Participles

Write the past participles.

Base Form	Simple Past	Past Participle
1. begin	began	*begun*
2. decide	decided	
3. fly	flew	
4. go	went	
5. hear	heard	
6. keep	kept	
7. make	made	
8. ride	rode	
9. see	saw	
10. swim	swam	
11. travel	traveled	
12. work	worked	

EXERCISE 2: Affirmative Statements

Complete these statements. Use the present perfect form of the correct verbs from Exercise 1.

1. Julie _____ *has made* _____ several trips this year.

2. You _____ on a camel. Did you enjoy it?

3. I'd like to go to Costa Rica. I _____ that it's beautiful.

4. They _____ the ancient Egyptian pyramids before.

5. He _____ Air France many times. It's his favorite airline.

6. I _____ with dolphins in the ocean. What an adventure!

7. My cousin _____ to go hiking in northern Spain next fall.

8. She _____ hard this year and really needs a vacation.

Read this article about a famous series of travel guides. Complete the sentences with the present perfect form of the verbs in parentheses.

Around the World with *Lonely Planet*

The Wheelers

As you probably know, travel ____*has become*____
1. (become)
very, very popular. As a result, hundreds of travel guides

_____ on bookstore shelves. One of the
2. (appear)

most popular travel-guide series is *Lonely Planet*, started

by Tony and Maureen Wheeler in the 1970s. The British

husband-and-wife team _____ always really _____
3. (love)

traveling, and they _____. They still make a lot of trips all over the
4. (not stop)

world. The first *Lonely Planet* guidebook was the result of one of their first trips.

Today, the series has more than 500 guidebooks, and Tony Wheeler

_____ and _____ many of them. The Wheelers
5. (research) **6. (write)**

_____ both _____ awards for their work, and *The New*
7. (receive)

York Times _____ Tony as "the most influential man in travel."
8. (describe)

Recently, *Lonely Planet* _____ a new partner. The British
9. (find)

Broadcasting Corporation now owns 75 percent of the company. The BBC

_____ to remain true to the goals of *Lonely Planet*—to give honest
10. (promise)

information and advice to independent travelers. The Wheelers themselves

_____ less active. In fact, they _____ the number of
11. (not become) **12. (increase)**

trips they make, and Tony _____ to write.
13. (continue)

Lonely Planet books are quite different from other guidebooks. The travel series

_____ always _____ travelers to do and explore new
14. (encourage)

things—not just the "Top-Ten Tourist Sights." If you _____ a *Lonely*
15. (not read)

Planet guide, check one out. We promise you: It will be an adventure—even if you

never leave your armchair!

EXERCISE 4: Questions and Answers with Adverbs and Time Expressions

A travel agent is talking to a client. Complete the travel agent's questions with the words in parentheses. Use the agent's notes and the correct adverb or time expression from the box to answer the questions. You will use some words more than once.

many times	never	not lately	once	recently	twice

Adventure Travel Inc.

Egypt — 2 X
Europe — more than 10 X
African safari — (returned two months ago)
Costa Rica — 1 X (2004)
China — no

hot-air ballooning — no
dolphin swim — 6 X or more

group tour — no (and _not_ interested)

1. **AGENT:** Have you ever been _____ to Egypt?
   (ever / be)

   CLIENT: I've been to Egypt twice. _____

2. **AGENT:** _____ Europe?
   (How many times / visit)

   CLIENT: _____

3. **AGENT:** _____ on an African safari?
   (ever / be)

   CLIENT: _____

4. **AGENT:** _____ to Costa Rica?
   (ever / be)

   CLIENT: _____

5. **AGENT:** _____ there?
   (How often / be)

   CLIENT: _____

(continued on next page)

6. AGENT: _____ in China?
                                    (travel)

CLIENT: _____

7. AGENT: _____ in a hot-air balloon?
                                  (ever / go up)

CLIENT: _____

8. AGENT: _____ with dolphins?
                                  (ever / swim)

CLIENT: _____

9. AGENT: _____ a group tour?
                                  (ever / take)

CLIENT: _____.
     And I never want to!

EXERCISE 5: Editing

Read these questions and answers posted on a travel website. There are nine mistakes in the use of the present perfect and adverbs. The first one is already corrected. Find and correct eight more.

⊙ ○ ○

TRAVEL WITH CAL

ever been
Q: Have you ~~been ever~~ to Barcelona? I'm planning a trip there this summer and would love some tips.

A: I've never been there, but you can find a lot of useful information on websites such as tripadvisor.com.

Q: I've returned last week from a safari in Africa. It was awesome, and I'm really interested in sharing photos with other travelers. Any ideas?

A: Yes! We've recently formed an online discussion group on safaris and we post photos there. Contact me at travcal@oal.com for more information.

Q: I'm trying to choose a hotel for my trip to Toronto. Has anyone you know ever stays at the Victoria?

A: I've several times stayed there myself. It's convenient and affordable. I think you'd like it.

Q: I'm going to be traveling alone in the south of France. What's the best form of transportation for getting around? I can't afford to rent a car.

A: I've always took local busses. They're comfortable and you get to see a lot of the countryside.

Q: Have you read the results of Travel Today's annual survey? It seems like a lot of people has decided to take vacations closer to home. And many people have choose not to go away at all this summer.

A: Not me! I've booked just a vacation to Australia. I've never was to that part of the world, and I can't wait to go!

EXERCISE 6: Personal Writing

Write a paragraph about your own travel experiences. Use the present perfect with some of the words from the box.

always	just	many times	never	not . . . lately	often	recently	twice

EXAMPLE: *There are so many places I would like to visit. I've never been to Asia, and I've always wanted to see . . .*

_____

_____

_____

_____

_____

_____

_____

_____

_____

_____

_____

_____

_____

Present Perfect and Simple Past

EXERCISE 1: Spelling: Regular and Irregular Verbs

Write the correct form of the verb.

Base Form	Simple Past	Past Participle
1. be	was / were	*been*
2. _____	became	become
3. begin	began	_____
4. _____	bought	bought
5. decide	_____	_____
6. feel	_____	felt
7. _____	_____	gotten
8. give	_____	_____
9. go	_____	_____
10. have	_____	had
11. _____	lived	_____
12. _____	made	made
13. meet	_____	_____
14. move	_____	_____
15. pay	_____	_____
16. read	_____	_____
17. rise	rose	_____
18. _____	_____	seen
19. start	_____	_____
20. _____	_____	taken

EXERCISE 2: Present Perfect or Simple Past

Complete the sentences about Tom Dorsey, a teacher who is looking for a job in another city.

Last Year	This Year
1. Tom answered 20 employment ads.	_____*Tom has answered*_____ 30 ads.
2. _____*Tom had*_____ two job interviews.	Tom has had three job interviews.
3. Tom went on one out-of-town interview.	_____ on three out-of-town interviews.
4. _____ one job offer.	Tom has gotten three job offers.
5. Tom made $40,000.	_____ the same amount of money.
6. _____ a lot of interesting people.	Tom has met a lot of interesting people too.
7. Tom was sick once.	_____ sick twice.
8. _____ well.	Tom has looked tired.
9. _____ a new digital camera.	Tom has bought a DVD player.
10. Tom paid with cash.	_____ by credit card.
11. Tom read five books.	_____ two books.
12. Tom didn't manage to take a vacation.	_____ to take two short vacations. He's been to Florida and southern California.
13. Tom didn't give any parties.	_____ two parties.
14. _____ a little discouraged.	Tom has felt a lot more encouraged.

EXERCISE 3: Present Perfect or Simple Past

A journalist is interviewing a woman about marriage. Complete the interview with the correct form of the verbs in parentheses. Use the present perfect or the simple past.

INTERVIEWER: How long ___*have*___ you ___*been*___ married?
1. (be)

WOMAN: We _____ married in 2009, so we _____ married for just
2. (get)   3. (be)

a few years.

INTERVIEWER: And when _____ you _____ your first child?
4. (have)

WOMAN: Well, I _____ a mother pretty quickly. We _____
5. (become)   6. (have)

Stephanie 10 months after we _____ married.
7. (be)

INTERVIEWER: You say this isn't your first marriage. How long _____ your first

marriage _____?
8. (last)

WOMAN: About two years. We _____ in 2006.
9. (divorce)

INTERVIEWER: _____ the two of you _____ any kids?
10. (have)

WOMAN: No, we _____.
11.

INTERVIEWER: Do you still see your first husband?

WOMAN: Yes. We _____ to stay friends. In fact, I _____ him last
12. (manage)   13. (see)

week. He and Tom _____ friends too. It's a nice arrangement.
14. (become)

INTERVIEWER: _____ he _____?
15. (remarry)

WOMAN: No, he _____. But I'm sure it's just a temporary situation.
16.

INTERVIEWER: In your opinion, why _____ your first marriage _____?
17. (fail)

WOMAN: I think that we _____ married too young. We _____ each
18. (get)   19. (not know)

other well enough.

INTERVIEWER: Where _____ you _____ Tom?
20. (meet)

WOMAN: In Atlanta. We _____ both students there.
21. (be)

INTERVIEWER: And when _____ you _____ to Los Angeles?
22. (move)

WOMAN: Last year. Los Angeles is the third city we _____ in! Tom is a college
23. (live)

professor, and it's hard to find a permanent job these days. So, when he gets a job

offer, he really can't turn it down. We don't like moving so often, so I hope this is just a

temporary solution to the job problem.

Read some facts about the changing American family. Complete the sentences with the present perfect or simple past form of the verbs from the boxes.

begin	~~change~~	get	have

The American family ___*has changed*___ a lot in the past 50 years. In the 1960s, couples
                          1.

_____ to get married at an older age. They also _____ divorced more
        2.   **3.**

frequently than they ever did, and they _____ fewer children.
                                                4.

be	create	occur	rise

Age

In 1960, the average age for a first marriage for women _____ 20.3 and for men,
                                                                5.

22.8. Today it _____ to 25.3 for women and 26.7 for men. In the early 1960s, most
                    6.

divorces _____ among couples older than 45. Today people of all ages are getting
              7.

divorced at a very high rate. This, in part, _____ many single-parent homes.
                                                    8.

be	have	increase	start

Birth Rate

In the mid-1960s, birth rates _____ to drop. Then, almost 60 percent of women
                                      9.

_____ three or more children by the time they _____ in their late 30s.
        10.   **11.**

These days, 35 percent of women in the same age group have only two children. In addition, the

number of births to older women _____ greatly _____.
                                        12.

change	get	reach	stay

Living Arrangements

Before 1960, most children _____ in their parents' homes until they
                                  13.

_____ married. This pattern _____ since then. Today many single
        14.   **15.**

people live alone. Also affecting today's living arrangements is the fact that life expectancy

_____ an all-time high of 78.2 years. This means that there are a lot more older
        16.

people, and some of them are moving in with their adult children.

EXERCISE 5: Editing

Read the student's email to a friend. There are eight mistakes in the use of the present perfect and the simple past. The first mistake is already corrected. Find and correct seven more.

Hi, Jennifer—

      met
Last month, I ~~have met~~ the most wonderful guy. His name is Roger, and he's a student in my

night class. He lived here since 2007. Before that he lived in Detroit too, so we have a lot in

common. Roger has been married for five years but got divorced last April.

Roger and I managed to spend a lot of time together in spite of our busy schedules. Last week I

saw him every night, and this week we already gotten together three times after class. I find that I

miss him when we're apart!

Monday night we have seen a great movie. Did you see *The Purple Room*? It's playing now at all

the theaters.

We've decided to take a trip back to Detroit in the summer. Maybe we can get together. It would

be great to see you again. Please let me know if you'll be there.

Love,

Diana

P.S. Here's a photo of Roger that I've taken a few weeks ago.

Write one or two paragraphs about how your life has changed in the past few years. Use some of the phrases from the box with the present perfect or simple past.

Five years ago, . . .	Lately . . .
For the past two years, . . .	. . . since 2012
Last year . . .	This year . . .

EXAMPLE: *My life has really changed a lot in the past few years. Five years ago, I only had a few friends here, but since I . . .*

_____

_____

_____

_____

_____

_____

_____

_____

_____

_____

_____

_____

_____

EXERCISE 1: Present Perfect Progressive Statements

Read the information about Amanda and Pete Kelly. Write a sentence—affirmative or negative—that summarizes the information. Use the present perfect progressive with **since** *or* **for.**

1. It's 9:00. Amanda began working at 7:00. She is still working.

    Amanda has been working since 7:00 OR *for two hours.*

2. She is writing articles about global warming. She began a series last month.

    _____

3. Amanda and Pete used to live in New York. They left New York a few years ago.

    _____

4. They are now living in Toronto. They moved there in 2009.

    _____

5. They drive a fuel-efficient car. They got it last year.

    _____

6. Pete lost his job last year. He isn't working now.

    _____

7. Pete and Amanda are thinking of traveling to Africa. They began thinking about this last year.

    _____

8. Amanda is reading a lot about Africa. She started a few months ago.

    _____

9. Pete went back to school last month. He's studying zoology[1].

    _____

10. Amanda and Pete started looking for a new apartment a month ago. They're still looking.

    _____

---

[1] *zoology:* the scientific study of animals and their behavior

EXERCISE 2: Present Perfect Progressive or Present Perfect

Read the article about a famous Canadian scientist and environmentalist. Complete the information with the present perfect progressive or present perfect form of the verbs in parentheses. If both forms are possible, use the present perfect progressive.

Making a World of Difference

Born in 1936 in Vancouver, Canada, David Suzuki is a

well-known scientist and a radio and TV broadcaster.[1] He

_____ *has* _____ also _____ *become* _____

1. (become)

one of the most famous environmentalists in the world. He

_____ more than 40 books about

2. (write)

nature and the environment, including books on these topics

for children. In acknowledgement of his accomplishments,

he _____ many awards, among them the United Nations Environmental

3. (win)

Program medal. Suzuki holds several academic degrees and is an expert in the fields of genetics (the

study of how the qualities of living things are passed on through the genes) and zoology (the study of

animals and their behavior). He taught for many years before retiring in 2001. Since his retirement,

he _____ professor emeritus[2] at the University of British Columbia. In

4. (be)

addition, he _____ more than 20 honorary degrees[3] for his work.

5. (receive)

In 1990, he started the David Suzuki Foundation. One of the organization's goals is to educate

people about environmental issues and encourage them to change behaviors that are harmful to

the Earth. For over two decades, the foundation _____ to protect Canada's

6. (work)

climate and to reverse global warming. It also _____ young people about

7. (teach)

the importance of a healthy environment.

On the Foundation's website there are suggestions of everyday actions that people can take to

help the environment. Suzuki himself _____ steps to help save the planet.

8. (take)

(continued on next page)

---

[1] **broadcaster:** someone who speaks on radio and television programs

[2] **professor emeritus:** a professor who is no longer working but still has an official title

[3] **honorary degree:** a degree a college or university gives to someone famous who did not take the courses necessary to receive the degree at the school

Lately, in order to use less fuel, he _____ going on vacations that require
9. (stop)

air travel. He _____ also _____ his speaking engagements so
10. (organize)

that they are geographically close, again saving fuel in getting from one place to another.

Above all, Suzuki is probably most famous for his work in television. In his long career, he

_____ and _____ many shows that teach
11. (design) **12. (develop)**

audiences about the wonders of our world. And for over 30 years, people in more than 40 countries

around the world _____ him as the host of the very popular TV series
13. (watch)

The Nature of Things.

Now in his seventies, Suzuki _____ classes at the university, but he
14. (not teach)

_____ educating people about nature and the results of climate change.
15. (not stop)

He strongly believes that global warming is a very serious problem, caused by human activities,

and that people must change their behaviors to save the planet. To spread his message, he

_____ and _____ speeches. By focusing people's
16. (travel) **17. (give)**

attention on environmental issues through his teaching, writings, speeches, and shows, David

Suzuki _____ a long way in fulfilling his foundation's mission: "to protect
18. (go)

the diversity of nature and our quality of life, now and for the future."

*David Suzuki's Foundation has suggestions of things people can do to help the environment. Read the list. Amanda and Pete have checked (✓) the things they do. Write sentences about what they **have done** or **haven't done** and what they **have been doing** or **haven't been doing**. Use the present perfect progressive or present perfect.*

Ten Little Things for Big Change

☐ 1. Buy locally grown and produced food.

☑ 2. Eat meat-free meals one day a week.

☐ 3. Don't use pesticides.[1]

☑ 4. Choose energy-efficient appliances.

☑ 5. Reduce home heating and electricity use.

☐ 6. Recycle paper, cans, and bottles.

☑ 7. Buy a fuel-efficient car.

☐ 8. Walk, bike, car pool, or take public transportation.

☐ 9. Choose a home close to work or school.

☐ 10. Take a vacation close to home.

_____

[1] *pesticide:* a chemical that kills insects

1. *They haven't been buying locally grown and produced food.*

2. _____

3. _____

4. _____

5. _____

6. _____

7. _____

8. _____

9. _____

10. _____

EXERCISE 4: Questions and Answers: Present Perfect Progressive or Present Perfect

Write questions about David Suzuki. Use the words in parentheses and the present perfect progressive or present perfect. Answer the questions with the information from Exercise 2.

1. (How many books / Suzuki / write)

How many books has Suzuki written?

He's written more than 40 books.

2. (he / win / any awards)

_____

_____

3. (How long / he / be retired)

_____

_____

4. (How many honorary degrees / he / receive)

_____

_____

5. (How long / his foundation / exist)

_____

_____

6. (What / the Foundation / teach / young people)

_____

_____

7. (What activity / Suzuki / stop)

_____

_____

8. (he / develop / a lot of TV shows)

_____

_____

9. (How long / people / watch / *The Nature of Things*)

_____

_____

10. (What / Suzuki / do / to spread his message)

_____

_____

EXERCISE 5: Editing

Read the student's blog. There are nine mistakes in the use of the present perfect progressive and present perfect. The first mistake is already corrected. Find and correct eight more.

Friday, April 22 (Earth Day!)

It's the second week of the fall semester. I've ~~taken~~ *been taking* a course on environmental issues with Professor McCarthy. He's an expert on the subject of global warming, and he's already been writing two books on the topic. I think one of them has even been winning an award.

For the past two weeks, we've studying pollution and how the Earth's temperature have been getting warmer. As part of the course, we've been reading a lot of books on the environment. For example, I've just been finishing a book called *The Sacred Balance: Rediscovering Our Place in Nature* by David Suzuki. He's a well-known Canadian scientist and environmentalist. It was fascinating. Since then, I've also read his autobiography. I've only been reading about 50 pages of the book so far, but it seems interesting too. I'm really learning a lot in this course, and I've been started to change some of the things I do in order to help protect the planet.

EXERCISE 6: Personal Writing

What **have you done** *or* **have you been doing** *lately to help the environment? Write a paragraph. Use the list in Exercise 3 on page 73 or your own ideas. Use some of the phrases from the box.*

For several years, I . . .	I haven't been . . .
I have . . .	Lately . . .
I have been . . .	Since I read about global warming, I . . .
I haven't . . .	Since 2011 . . .

EXAMPLE: *Since I read about global warming, I've been trying to use less gasoline. For example, I've started . . .*

_____

_____

_____

_____

_____

_____

_____

_____

_____

UNIT 13 Ability: *Can, Could, Be able to*

EXERCISE 1: Affirmative and Negative Statements with *Can* and *Could*

Read about a student's ability in English. Then complete the statements for each item. (For items 8–10, write complete statements.) Use **can, can't, could,** *or* **couldn't.**

Student's Name Fernando Ochoa

English Language Ability Questionnaire

Skill	Now	Before This Course
1. understand conversational English	✔	✘
2. understand recorded announcements	✘	✘
3. read an English newspaper	✔	✔
4. read an English novel	✘	✘
5. speak on the phone	✔	✘
6. speak with a group of people	✔	✘
7. write an email	✔	✔
8. write a business letter	✘	✘
9. order a meal in English	✔	✔
10. go shopping	✔	✔

1. Before this course, he _____ *couldn't understand conversational English* _____.

Now he _____ *can understand conversational English* _____.

2. He _____ *couldn't understand recorded announcements* _____ before the course, and

he still _____ *can't understand recorded announcements* _____.

3. He _____ now, and he

_____ before too.

(continued on next page)

4. He _____ before the course, and

he still _____.

5. Now he _____, but before the course

he _____.

6. Before the course, he _____, but

now he _____.

7. Before the course, he _____.

He still _____, of course.

8. _____

_____

9. _____

_____

10. _____

_____

SUMMARY: Fernando _____ do a lot more now than he

_____ before the course.

EXERCISE 2: Questions and Answers with *Can* and *Could*

A reporter from the school newspaper is interviewing a new student. Use **can** *or* **could** *and the words in parentheses to write the interview questions and the student's answers.*

1. (speak / any other languages)

REPORTER: _Can you speak any other languages?_____

STUDENT: _Yes, I can._____ I speak two other languages.

2. (What languages / speak)

REPORTER: _____

STUDENT: Spanish and French.

3. (speak Spanish / when you were a child)

REPORTER: _____

STUDENT: _____ I learned it as an adult.

4. (speak French)

REPORTER: _____

STUDENT: _____ We spoke French some of the time at home.

5. (before you came here / understand spoken English)

REPORTER: _____

STUDENT: _____ I didn't understand anything! I was always

confused. I hated it.

6. (understand song lyrics)

REPORTER: What about now? _____

STUDENT: _____ Especially if I listen to them more than once.

7. (before this course / write a business letter in English)

REPORTER: _____

STUDENT: _____ But I used to write in English to my friends.

8. (drive a car before you came here)

REPORTER: So, tell me some more about yourself. _____

STUDENT: _____ I was too young.

9. (drive a car now)

REPORTER: _____

STUDENT: _____ I still haven't learned.

10. (swim)

REPORTER: We're not far from the beach here. _____

STUDENT: _____ I've been swimming since I was a little kid.

11. (surf before you came here)

REPORTER: What about surfing? _____

STUDENT: _____ But I learned to surf the first month I was here.

12. (What / do now / that / you / not do before)

REPORTER: _____

STUDENT: Oh! I _____ a lot of things now that I

_____ before.

EXERCISE 3: Affirmative and Negative: *Can* and *Can't*

Complete the article about hearing loss with **can** *or* **can't** *and the correct words from the boxes.*

damage	~~hear~~	recover	survive

Some people _____ can't hear _____ as the result of a childhood illness, but many
                                  1.

people lose their hearing as a result of everyday exposure to loud noise. Very loud sounds

_____ the hair cells in your ear, which are necessary for hearing. These cells
               2.

_____ from mild damage, but they _____ severe
               3.   **4.**

damage, which kills them and causes permanent hearing loss.

be	do	leave	listen	lose	understand

Many people are exposed to loud noise at work. Construction workers, factory workers, and

firefighters are just a few examples. But did you know that you _____ your
                                                                              5.

hearing from iPods™ and other personal listening devices that you use with ear phones? In part

because of longer-lasting batteries, people _____ for hours without taking
                                                        6.

a break.

So, what _____ YOU _____ to protect your
                                                              7.

ears? Here are a few tips.

- Wear safety ear muffs or ear plugs if you work in a loud environment.

- Turn the volume down on your iPod or other personal listening devices.

- Don't sit near the band or loud speakers at a concert or party.

And be aware of the noise level in your environment. What's too loud? If you have to shout so

that someone near you _____ you, the noise level is dangerous. If you
                                    8.

_____ the area, take other steps to protect your ears. When it comes to your
               9.

hearing, you _____ too careful!
                        10.

EXERCISE 4: Affirmative and Negative Statements with *Be able to*

Read the article about hearing loss. Complete the article with the correct form of **be able to** and the verbs in parentheses.

Living in a Hearing World

There are millions of people who have some degree of hearing loss. There are two major types of hearing loss.

1. **Sound Sensitivity Loss.** People with this kind of loss _____are not able to hear_____
    1. (not hear)

    soft sounds—a whisper or a bird singing, for example. However, when sounds are loud

    enough, they _____ them correctly.
    2. (interpret)

2. **Sound Discrimination Loss.** People with this particular kind of hearing loss

    _____ one sound from another. As a result of this,
    3. (not distinguish)

    they _____ speech—even when it is loud enough
    4. (not understand)

    for them to hear.

    How do people with hearing disabilities get along in a hearing world? Most people with

hearing impairments _____ some sounds. With the use
5. (hear)

of hearing aids and cochlear implants (devices put in the ear during an operation), many

people _____ some of their ability to hear. Some people
6. (get back)

with hearing disabilities _____ lips. But, at best, lip-reading
7. (read)

is only 30 to 50 percent effective. Even a good lip-reader _____
8. (not recognize)

all the sounds. Just ask someone to silently mouth the words *pat*, *bat*, and *mat*. The three

words sound different, but they all *look* the same when someone says them. In addition, the

human eye _____ fast enough to process speech by
9. (not work)

vision alone. By far the most successful form of communication is signing—the use of sign

language. People with hearing impairments _____
10. (communicate)

successfully with others who know this language.

EXERCISE 5: Questions and Short Answers with *Be able to*

*Modern technology can make life easier for people with hearing loss. Read this FAQ (frequently asked questions) about assisted-hearing devices. Use **will be able to** to complete the questions and write short answers.*

Q: My daughter has a hearing disability. She's going to have her first child next month.

_____Will_____ she _____be able to know_____ when the baby is crying?
　　　　　　　　　　　　　1. (know)

A: _____Yes, she will._____ She can get a device that flashes lights (so she'll be
　　　　　　　2.

able to see the signal) or vibrates (so she'll be able to feel the signal).

　　　　　　　　　　　　　　　　　******

Q: My nephew can't hear the alarm clock in the morning. I want to buy him a flashing lamp.

_____ he _____ it when he's sleeping?
　　　　　　　　　　　　3. (how / see)

A: You can see a strong light through your eyelids—as long as you don't have your head under

the covers!

　　　　　　　　　　　　　　　　　******

Q: I'm thinking of getting a cochlear implant. _____ I _____
　　　　　　　　　　　　　　　　　　　　　　　　　　　　　　4. (hear)

"normally" with it?

A: _____ Hearing with an implant is not the same as
　　　　　　　5.

"normal" hearing, but it *can* help a lot.

　　　　　　　　　　　　　　　　　******

Q: I just moved into a new apartment, and I'm having trouble hearing the doorbell.

_____ I _____ this problem without
　　　　　　　　　　　　6. (how / solve)

disturbing my neighbors?

A: You can get a system that produces sound in different locations in your apartment—not just

at the front door.

　　　　　　　　　　　　　　　　　******

Q: My husband and I both wear hearing aids, and we both love to travel. _____ we

_____ the theater when we're in London next summer?
　　　　　　　7. (enjoy)

A: _____ Theaters in London use a "loop" system. This
　　　　　　　8.

system sends sounds directly to your hearing aid (without wires!). You just need to set your

hearing aid to "T." Have a good trip!

EXERCISE 6: Contrast: *Can* and *Be able to*

Read the article about a well-known actress who is deaf. Complete the story with the correct form of **can, could,** *or* **be able to** *and the verbs in parentheses. Use* **can** *or* **could** *when possible.*

Actress Marlee Matlin _____*could hear*_____ at birth but
1. (hear)

lost her hearing at the age of eighteen months as a result of a childhood

illness. By the age of five, she _____ lips. Shortly
2. (read)

after that, she mastered sign language. At first, Matlin felt angry and

frightened by her hearing impairment. "I wanted to be perfect, and I

_____ my deafness," she said during an interview.
3. (not accept)

With time, however, she learned to accept it.

Matlin began her acting career at the age of eight, when she performed in theater for the deaf. It

was clear from the start that she had a lot of talent. In 1986, she received an Oscar award for best

actress in the Hollywood film *Children of a Lesser God*. In the movie, she played the role of an angry

woman who was deaf and did not want to speak. For Matlin, however, speaking is very important.

At the Oscar ceremonies, she _____ her award verbally. It was the first
4. (accept)

time the public heard her speak. "It's what I wanted to do, because a lot of people all over the world

_____ me for who I am," she said. Matlin was worried, however. She asked,
5. (see)

"What other roles _____ I _____ in the future?"
6. (do)

Matlin didn't need to worry. She continued to receive important roles in movies and on

TV. Her work has helped changed people's perceptions of what deaf people can and cannot

do. One reviewer said "She _____ more saying nothing than most
7. (do)

people _____ talking." Today, thanks to intensive speech training
8. (do)

and a lot of dedication, she _____ very clearly. In 1994, she
9. (speak)

_____ something for the first time: She played the role of a character
10. (achieve)

who was not deaf. Matlin, in fact, doesn't think of herself as a "deaf actress." She's an "actress who

happens to be deaf." One of her aspirations is that in the future she _____
11. (get)

more roles that are not specifically for people with hearing impairments.

(continued on next page)

In addition to her acting career, Matlin is actively trying to improve lives. In 1995, she helped get an important law passed in the United States. As a result of this law, today most TV sets have closed-captioning on their screens so that hearing-impaired viewers _____

12. (read)

everything. Matlin does not believe in limits. "I _____ attitudes on deafness

13. (change)

and prove we _____ everything—except hear," she said.

14. (do)

EXERCISE 7: Editing

Read the student's composition. There are nine mistakes in the use of **can, could,** *and* **be able to.** *The first one is already corrected. Find and correct eight more.*

                          couldn't

Before I came to this country, I ~~can't~~ do many things in English. For example I couldn't follow a conversation if many people were talking at the same time. I always got confused. I remember a party I went to. Everyone was speaking English, and I wasn't able understand a word! I felt so uncomfortable. Finally, my aunt came to pick me up, and I could leave the party.

Today I can to understand much better. I am taking classes at the adult center. My teacher is very good. She can explains things well, and she always gives us the chance to talk a lot in class. When I finish this class in May, I can speak and understand a lot better.

Speaking English well is very important to me. I practice a lot at home too. When I first came to this country, I can't understand very much TV, but now I can to understand much better. In fact, I can do a lot now, and I think in a few more months I can do even more.

EXERCISE 8: Personal Writing

Look at the English Language Ability Questionnaire in Exercise 1 on page 77. Write a paragraph about your English ability now and before this course. Use **can, can't, could, couldn't,** *and* **be able to.**

EXAMPLE: My English has improved quite a lot. Before I started studying here, I couldn't understand conversational English very much at all, but now I'm able to understand a lot more. For example, I can . . .

_____

_____

_____

_____

_____

_____

_____

_____

_____

_____

_____

EXERCISE 1: Questions and Responses

Match the classroom questions and responses.

Questions	Responses
_d_ **1.** Do you mind if I bring my friends to class?	**a.** Certainly. The key to the rest room is hanging on the wall.
_____ **2.** May I ask a question?	**b.** Not at all. I think it's a good idea.
_____ **3.** Do you mind if I record the class?	**c.** Sure. I hope I can answer it.
_____ **4.** Could I open the window?	~~**d.**~~ Sorry. It's already pretty crowded.
_____ **5.** Can we review Unit 4?	**e.** Sure. But remember: You don't have to look up every word.
_____ **6.** May I leave the room?	**f.** I'm afraid we can't. We're out of time.
_____ **7.** Could we use our dictionaries?	**g.** Sure. But please remember to return it.
_____ **8.** Could I borrow a pen?	**h.** Go right ahead. It's quite warm in here.

EXERCISE 2: Questions

Read the classroom situations. Complete the questions asking for permission.

1. You want to open the window.

May _I open the window?_ _____

2. Your whole class wants to review Unit 6.

Could _____

3. You want to borrow a classmate's pen.

Can _____

4. You want to look at someone's class notes.

Do you mind if _____

5. You want to come late to the next class.

Do you mind if _____

6. Your roommate wants to come to the next class with you.

Could _____

7. You want to ask a question.

May _____

8. You and a classmate would like to use a dictionary.

Can _____

9. You and your classmates want to leave five minutes early.

Could _____

10. Your sister wants to go on the class trip with the rest of the class.

Do you mind if _____

EXERCISE 3: Affirmative and Negative Statements

Look at the flyer. Complete the statements with the words in parentheses.

Class Trip

You are invited to our annual class picnic on

Sunday, May 26, at Glenwood State Park

Food and beverages welcome, but no glass containers, please!

Bus tickets $5.00 (check or cash)

Advance purchase only • No refunds

Bring a friend!

Don't forget your bathing suit! The lake is beautiful.

1. You _____*may bring*_____ a friend.
    (may / bring)

2. You _____ your own food.
    (can / bring)

3. You _____ your own drinks.
    (can / bring)

4. You _____ juice from a glass bottle at the picnic.
    (can / drink)

5. You _____ for your bus ticket by check.
    (can / pay)

6. You _____ for your bus ticket by cash.
    (can / pay)

7. You _____ for your ticket by credit card.
    (may / pay)

(continued on next page)

8. You _____ your bus ticket on the day of the trip.
(may / purchase)

9. You _____ a refund.
(can / get)

10. You _____ in the lake.
(may / swim)

EXERCISE 4: Editing

*Read the professor's response to an email from one of his students. (The professor's answers are in **bold print**.) There are six mistakes in making and responding to requests. The first one is already corrected. Find and correct five more.*

Subj: Missed classes—Reply
Date: 04-23-12 11:22:43 EST
From: profwilson@bryant.edu
To: Timbotwo@hotline.com

Professor Wilson—

I've been sick for the past two days. That's why I missed the last test. I'm really annoyed.
                                                                      take
I studied a lot for it and was really well prepared. May I ~~taking~~ a make-up exam?

I know you never miss class, Tim, so I assumed that's what happened. I hope you're

feeling better. Yes, you can take a make-up exam if you bring a doctor's note.

If I can take the exam, may I use my calculator during the test?

No, you mayn't! It's against the guidelines we established at the beginning of the

semester. Remember?

Could my roommate comes to class and take notes for me on Thursday?

Yes, he could. I hope you can read his handwriting!

Do you mind when he records Allison's presentation for me? I don't want to miss it.

Not at all. It's fine for him to record the presentation.

One last thing—I know I missed some handouts. May I have please copies of them?

Sure. I'll give them to your roommate on Thursday.

Thanks a lot.

Tim

EXERCISE 5: Personal Writing

Write an email to your teacher asking for permission to do something. Use at least two of the situations from the box (or your own ideas). Use **can I, could I, may I,** *and* **do you mind if.**

> You've been having difficulty understanding what the teacher is saying.
>
> You're feeling sick and need to miss class.
>
> Your cousin (from your country) is going to visit you for a week.
>
> You're having trouble with a paper you're writing.
>
> You'd like to use your calculator during your math test.

EXAMPLE: Dear Ms. Johnson,

I'm not feeling well and I'm going to have to miss our next class. I know you're giving a test that day. Could I take the test next week instead of on Wednesday? Also, at the end of the month, my cousin . . .

_____

_____

_____

_____

_____

_____

_____

_____

_____

_____

_____

_____

15 Requests: *Can, Could, Will, Would, Would you mind*

EXERCISE 1: Requests and Responses

Match the office requests and responses.

Requests

___d___ **1.** Could you meet me tomorrow at 8:00 A.M.?

_____ **2.** Will you please type this memo for me?

_____ **3.** Could you show me how to use the scanner?

_____ **4.** Would you please spell your last name for me?

_____ **5.** Would you mind distributing this report for me?

_____ **6.** Can you cancel tomorrow's meeting for me? I have to go out of town.

_____ **7.** Will you shut the window, please?

_____ **8.** Would you get that box down from the closet? I'd really appreciate it.

_____ **9.** Could you get the phone for me?

_____ **10.** Can you give me Doug Johnson's email address?

Responses

a. I'd be glad to. When do you need it?

b. Sure. It is pretty cold in here.

c. Of course I can. When would you like to reschedule it?

d. I'm sorry. I have an early-morning dentist appointment.

e. Sure. It's Djohn@iol.com.

f. Sure. . . . Hello, J and R Equities.

g. Sure. It's M-A-R-D-J-A-I-T.

h. Sorry, but I don't know how. Ask Todd. He knows how.

i. I'd like to, but it's too heavy for me to lift.

j. Not at all.

Write the letters of the responses that mean "Yes": __a,_____

Write the letters of the responses that mean "No": _____

Write the letter of the response that has a negative word, but means

"OK, I'll do it.": _____

EXERCISE 2: Requests

These conversations take place in an office. Use the correct form of the phrases from the box to complete the requests.

~~answer the phone~~	keep the noise down
buy some stamps	lend me $5.00
come to my office	open the window
explain this note to me	pick up a sandwich
get Frank's phone number	stay late tonight

1. **A:** Could you _____ *answer the phone* _____? My hands are full.

   B: Sure. I'll get it.

2. **A:** Would you mind _____? It's really hot in here.

   B: No, not at all.

3. **A:** Can you please _____ for me?

   B: Certainly. I pass the post office on my way home.

4. **A:** I'm going to the coffee shop. Can I get you anything?

   B: Could you _____ for me?

5. **A:** Would you mind _____? We really have to get this

   report done by tomorrow.

   B: I'm sorry, but I have to visit my aunt in the hospital.

6. **A:** Will you _____, please? I can't hear myself think!

   B: Sorry!

7. **A:** Can you _____ when you have the chance?

   B: Sure. I'll be right there.

8. **A:** Would you _____ for me?

   B: It's 555–4345.

9. **A:** Would you mind _____?

   B: Not at all. What don't you understand?

10. **A:** Could you _____?

    B: Oh, I'm sorry. I'm short on cash.

EXERCISE 3: Word Order

Unscramble the words to make requests. Use the correct form of the verbs.

1. come / can / please / here / you

   Can you please come here?

2. work / on Saturday / would you mind

3. you / me / please / will / help

4. would / please / text / you / your decision / me

5. drive / home / you / me / please / could

EXERCISE 4: Editing

Read the office messages. There are six mistakes in making requests. The first mistake is already corrected. Find and correct five more. Don't forget to check punctuation.

1.

> Meng,
>
> Would you ~~filed~~ file these, please?
>
> Thanks,
>
> R. L.

2.

> write it down
>
> Hi, Ted,
>   Could you please remember to turn off the lights when you leave?
>   Thanks,
>   Lynn

3.

HANK,

WILL YOU RETURN PLEASE THE STAPLER?

BRAD

4.

Melida,

Can you make 5 copies of these pages, please?

Thanks,

Ellen

5.

John,

Would you mind deliver the finished report to me before you leave for the day?

Rey

6.

Celia,
Could you please remember to lock the door.
Thank you.

Diana

7.

Annie,
Would you please to call Ms. Rivera before the end of the day?

Thanks,
JG

8.

Todd—
Could you print out 10 copies of the Hendricks report?
Also, would you mind to email Lisa Barker a copy? That'll cheer her up!

Thanks a lot.
Heather

EXERCISE 5: Personal Writing

Write a note to someone you live with. Make at least three requests with **can, could, will, would,** *or* **would you mind.** *Use some of the situations from the box or ones of your own.*

the building manager has called twice	the living room is messy
the dishes are dirty	the plants need watering
the electric bill hasn't been paid	the refrigerator is almost empty

EXAMPLE: *Hi, Brian,*

I've got to leave for school now and I won't be back until after 8:00 tonight. Could you please wash the dishes? Also, the refrigerator is almost empty. We need some food in the house. Would you . . . ?

_____

_____

_____

_____

_____

_____

_____

_____

_____

_____

_____

Rewrite the cell-phone tips. Give advice with **should**. *Choose between affirmative and negative.*

CELL-PHONE ETIQUETTE

Cell phones have made communication a lot easier, but they can also be very annoying. Here are some rules you should follow to be polite.

■ Turn off your cell phone in public places such as movie theaters and class.

1. *You should turn off your cell phone in public places such as movie theaters and class.*

■ Don't shout into the phone.

2. _____

■ Speak in a quiet, normal voice.

3. _____

■ Leave the room to make a phone call.

4. _____

■ Don't discuss private issues in public places. Protect your own and other people's privacy.

5. _____

■ Don't stand too close to other people when you are talking on the phone.

6. _____

■ Pay attention to other people on the street when you are walking and talking.

7. _____

■ Never use a cell phone when you are driving. Even hands-free phones are dangerous.

8. _____

EXERCISE 2: Affirmative and Negative Statements with *Should, Ought to, Had better*

Complete the conversations with the correct form of the verbs in parentheses. Choose between affirmative and negative. Use contractions when possible.

1. **A:** Excuse me, but you really _____*shouldn't use*_____ your cell phone in here. The
   (should / use)

   sign says, "No cell phones."

   B: Sorry. I didn't see the sign.

2. **A:** You _____ Aunt Rosa. I know she'd be happy to hear from you.
   (should / call)

   B: Good idea. I'll call her as soon as I get off the phone with you.

3. **A:** You _____ to pick up some milk on the way home. We're all out
   (had better / forget)

   of it, and we need it for dinner.

   B: Call me again to remind me. OK?

4. **A:** We _____ the movie at Cinema Village Saturday night. I hear it's
   a. (ought to / see)

   really great.

   B: OK. But we _____ tickets sometime in the afternoon, or it'll be
   b. (had better / buy)

   hard to get in.

   A: Maybe we _____ them online. That way we can avoid standing *in*
   c. (should / get)

   line! I just hate waiting in line.

5. **A:** We _____ that restaurant near the theater.
   (should / try)

   B: Good idea. I'll call and make a reservation.

6. **A:** Our cell-phone bill is really high. I think we _____ about
   a. (ought to / think)

   changing calling plans.

   B: You're right. We _____ it.
   b. (should / look into)

7. **A:** People really _____ on their cell phones while they're driving. It's
   a. (should / talk)

   very dangerous behavior.

   B: You know, it's illegal in many places.

   A: Well, there _____ a law against it here too.
   b. (should / be)

8. **A:** You _____ Andy now. He's probably already asleep.
   (had better / call)

   B: OK. I'll call him tomorrow.

9. A: They _____ a "quiet car" on this train. It's hard to work with all
(ought to / have)

these people talking on their cells.

B: That's a great idea.

10. A: I _____ call-waiting on my cell phone. I'm missing too many
(should / get)

calls without it.

B: I'm surprised you don't have it already.

11. A: I _____ caller ID too.
(ought to / have)

B: Absolutely. It's important to know the identity of the person calling you.

12. A: I _____ so loud. I think I'm disturbing people around me.
(should / talk)

B: Just call me when you get home. OK?

13. A: It's 7:00. I _____ now. I don't want to be late.
(had better / hang up)

B: OK. Talk to you later.

EXERCISE 3: Questions and Answers with *Should*

Read the invitation. Use the words in parentheses and the information in the invitation to complete the phone conversation.

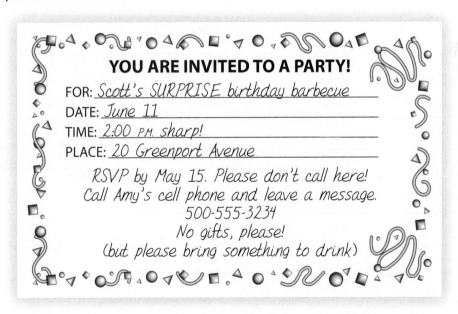

YOU ARE INVITED TO A PARTY!
FOR: *Scott's SURPRISE birthday barbecue*
DATE: *June 11*
TIME: *2:00 P.M. sharp!*
PLACE: *20 Greenport Avenue*
RSVP by May 15. Please don't call here!
Call Amy's cell phone and leave a message.
500-555-3234
No gifts, please!
(but please bring something to drink)

LISA: Hi, Tania.

TANIA: Hi, Lisa. What's up?

LISA: Aunt Rosa's having a birthday party for Uncle Scott. She didn't have your new address, so

she asked me to call and invite you. It's on June 11. Can you come?

(continued on next page)

Advice: *Should, Ought to, Had better* **97**

TANIA: Sure. Just give me all the information. (What time / be there)

What time should I be there?

1.

LISA: Let's see. I have the invitation right here.

You should be there at 2:00 P.M. sharp.

2.

TANIA: (What / wear)

_____

3.

LISA: Something casual. It's a barbecue.

TANIA: (bring a gift)

_____

4.

LISA: _____ The invitation says, "No gifts."

5.

TANIA: OK. What about food? (bring something to eat or drink)

_____

6.

LISA: _____

7.

Oh, and the invitation says, "RSVP." In other words, Aunt Rosa wants a response.

TANIA: (When / respond)

_____

8.

LISA: _____

9.

TANIA: (call Aunt Rosa)

_____

10.

LISA: _____ I forgot to tell you. It's a *surprise* party!

11.

TANIA: OK. (Who / call)

_____

12.

LISA: _____

13.

TANIA: Fine. Sounds like fun. I'll see you there. Thanks for calling.

LISA: No problem. See you there.

Read the quiz. There are eleven mistakes in the use of **should, ought to,** *and* **had better.** *The first mistake is already corrected. Find and correct ten more.*

Party Etiquette Quiz

Do you know what you should do at a party? Check (✔) the best answer.

1. You are at a party and you can't remember someone's name. What ~~you should~~ *should you* do?

   ☐ **a.** You should no ask the person's name.

   ☐ **b.** You better avoid the person or leave immediately

   ☐ **c.** You ought just ask.

2. You don't know anyone at the party, and your host doesn't introduce you to the other guests. Had you better introduce yourself?

   ☐ **a.** Yes, you should. You should say, "Hi. My name's _____."

   ☐ **b.** No, you should. You'd better tell the host to introduce you.

3. Your cell phone rings during the party. You should answer it?

   ☐ **a.** Just let it ring. You had not better answer it.

   ☐ **b.** You should answer it, but just have a short conversation.

   ☐ **c.** You really ought to leave the room and speak to the person in private.

4. You had a very nice time at the party. How you should thank your host?

   ☐ **a.** You should just say "thank you" when you leave.

   ☐ **b.** You should send a "thank-you" email the next day.

   ☐ **c.** You oughta write a long "thank-you" letter and send a gift too.

5. Everyone brought gifts to the party. You didn't.

   ☐ **a.** You'd better to apologize right away.

   ☐ **b.** You shouldn't say anything, but you ought to send a gift later.

   ☐ **c.** You should leave immediately and go buy a gift.

EXERCISE 5: Personal Writing

Imagine that a friend of yours is going to a party. He or she won't know anyone there and feels a little nervous. Write an email giving your friend advice. Use some of the phrases from the box.

You really should . . .	You shouldn't . . .
You ought to . . .	You'd better not . . .
You'd better . . .	Maybe you should . . .

EXAMPLE: *Hi, Hannah,*

Stop worrying! I'm sure you'll have a good time at the party. I think you should just relax and try to be yourself. Before you go, you ought to . . .

_____

_____

_____

_____

_____

_____

_____

_____

_____

_____

_____

EXERCISE 1: Nouns

A. *Read the article about an ancient Egyptian king. Underline the nouns.*

TUT'S TOMB[1]: AN EGYPTIAN TIME CAPSULE

Tutankhamun, better known as King Tut, became king of ancient Egypt when he was only nine years old. He died before his nineteenth birthday around 1323 B.C.E., and was mostly forgotten. Thousands of years later, British archeologist Howard Carter searched for his tomb. In 1922, after searching for many years, he finally found it near the Nile River, across from the modern Egyptian city of Luxor. Inside he discovered thousands of items buried along with the young king. Among the many treasures[2] were:

- furniture—including couches and chairs
- jewelry—including bracelets and necklaces
- clothing—including gloves, scarves, and shoes
- musical instruments
- chariots[3]
- vases and jars
- pots made of clay[4] (they probably once contained money)
- games and toys (Tut played with them as a child)
- food and wine
- gold

Tut's tomb is a time capsule. It gives us a picture of how Egyptian kings lived more than 3000 years ago, how they died, and what they expected to need in their lives after death.

Since his discovery, Tut has not been resting in peace. He and his treasures have traveled to exhibitions around the world, where millions of visitors have been able to view some of the wonders[5] of his ancient civilization.

[1] **tomb:** a place where a dead body is buried; ancient Egyptian kings' tombs were very large and often had several rooms
[2] **treasure:** valuable and important objects such as gold and jewelry
[3] **chariot:** an ancient form of transportation made of wood with two wheels and pulled by a horse
[4] **clay:** heavy soil that is soft when wet, but hard when dry or baked
[5] **wonder:** an amazing thing

B. *Put the nouns from the article into the correct columns. Choose only sixteen count nouns.*

Proper Nouns	Common Nouns			
	Count Nouns		Non-Count Nouns	
1. ___Tut___	1. ___tomb___ 9. _____		1. ___furniture___ 6. _____	
2. _____	2. _____ 10. _____		2. _____ 7. _____	
3. _____	3. _____ 11. _____		3. _____ 8. _____	
4. _____	4. _____ 12. _____		4. _____ 9. _____	
5. _____	5. _____ 13. _____		5. _____ 10. _____	
6. _____	6. _____ 14. _____			
7. _____	7. _____ 15. _____			
	8. _____ 16. _____			

EXERCISE 2: Noun and Verb Agreement

Complete the fact sheet with the correct form of the words in parentheses.

Did You Know . . . ?

The Pyramids

▲ Egypt's official _____name is_____ the Arab Republic
　　　　　　　　1. (name / be)

of Egypt.

▲ The _____ in northeastern Africa and
　　　2. (country / lie)

southwestern Asia.

▲ About 17,000,000 _____ in Cairo, the capital of Egypt. It's the 11th largest
　　　　　　　　3. (people / live)

city in the world.

▲ _____ many interesting sites for tourists to visit, including many pyramids.
　　4. (Cairo / have)

▲ _____ one of the most important export crops. _____ in
　　5. (cotton / be)　　　　　　　　　　　　　　　　　　6. (rice / grow)

many parts of the country and is an important food crop.

▲ Most _____ Egypt during the months of October through May.
　　　7. (tourist / visit)

▲ The Islamic holy month of _____ at a different time each year.
　　　　　　　　　　8. (Ramadan / take place)

During Ramadan many _____.
　　　　　　　　9. (shop and restaurant / close)

▲ The _____ usually very hot in the summer. Cool, comfortable
　　10. (weather / be)

_____ important, and _____ a must.
　11. (clothing / be)　　　　　　　12. (sunhat / be)

EXERCISE 3: Quantifiers

Circle the correct words to complete this FAQ about traveling to Egypt.

Q: How many / (much) time should I spend in Cairo?
1.

A: There are so many / much things to do and see in this great city that you could easily
2.

spend a great deal of / several weeks there. Most people can't, though, so we recommend at
3.

least a little / a few days.
4.

Q: Do many / much people speak English?
5.

A: Yes. Arabic is the official language, but few / a lot of people speak English.
6.

Q: How many / much money should I take?
7.

A: In the big cities, many / few places accept credit cards, so you don't need to carry
8.

a little / much cash. There are also ATMs. But in smaller places, it's a good idea to have
9.

some / several cash or traveler's checks.
10.

Q: I'm thinking about renting a car. Is it easy to get around?

A: It's not a great idea to drive, especially in the cities. There is a lot of / several traffic. In the
11.

city, use a taxi. Cairo has a subway too.

Q: I'd like to go on a Nile River cruise. Can I book that once I'm in Egypt?

A: Yes. There are a few / few travel agencies in Cairo and Luxor that arrange tours that
12.

include boat trips.

Q: I'll need to buy any / some souvenirs to bring home. What do you recommend?
13.

A: You have little / a lot of great choices. It's always nice to bring back some / a few gold or
14.   15.

silver jewelry. You'll also find some / several beautiful cotton fabric. And don't forget to pick
16.

up some / any spices at one of the enough / many markets you'll see.
17.   18.

Q: This may seem like a strange question, but how did King Tut die?

A: Many / Much people ask that! For many / much years, historians believed Tut was killed.
19.   20.

Today there is several / a lot of evidence that he died as a result of a disease and severe
21.

injuries to his leg.

Read the posts to a travel website. There are sixteen mistakes in the use of nouns and in verb and pronoun agreement. The first mistake is already corrected. Find and correct fifteen more.

○ ○ ○

I can't tell you how much we enjoyed our trip to ~~egypt~~ *Egypt*. We just returned few days ago. What an amazing country! There are so much things to see and do. My only complaint are that we didn't have enough time! But, we'll be back!

Hannes Koch, Germany

We saw a lot of tombs and pyramids on our recent trip, but the best were the three Giza pyramids. It is huge! And, I was surprised to learn, they are located right at the edge of the city of Cairo. Because of this, there is a lot of traffic getting there (and back). There were also a lot tourists. The day we were there it was very hot. If you go, you should know that there are a few places to get anything to drink, so I REALLY recommend that you bring any water with you. Oh, and if you want to see the inside of a pyramid, you need a special ticket, and they only sell a little tickets each day. Get there early if you want one!

Vilma Ortiz, USA

The food are great in Egypt! We went to some wonderful Restaurants. We found out about one place near our hotel that doesn't have much tourists. Mostly local people eats there and everyone was really friendly. I particularly enjoyed the "meze" (a variety of appetizers). You choose a little different plates before you order your main dish. Delicious!

Jim Cook, England

There are many beautiful beach in Alexandria. A lot of them are private or connected to hotels, but there are also public ones, so be sure to bring a bathing suit if you visit that part of Egypt. The water were warm—like being in a bathtub!

Aki Kato, Japan

EXERCISE 5: Personal Writing

Imagine that you just came back from a trip. Write an email to a friend about the trip. Use some of the phrases from the box and ideas of your own.

I really liked . . .	The people . . .
I saw . . .	The weather . . .
The buildings . . .	There were . . .
The food . . .	We bought . . .

EXAMPLE: *Hi! I just got back from Lima, Peru! It's a really interesting city. The people are very friendly and . . .*

_____

_____

_____

_____

_____

_____

_____

_____

_____

_____

_____

EXERCISE 1: Indefinite and Definite Articles

Some people are talking in school. Circle the correct words to complete the conversations.
If you don't need an article, circle Ø.

1. **A:** Can I borrow (a) / the pen?

   B: Sure. Take <u>a / the</u> one on <u>a / the</u> desk. I don't need it.

2. **A:** Is <u>a / the</u> teacher here yet?

   B: No, she hasn't come yet.

3. **A:** What do you think of Mr. Mencz?

   B: He's wonderful. He's <u>a / the</u> best teacher I've ever had.

4. **A:** Have you done <u>the / Ø</u> homework?

   B: Yes. But I don't think I got <u>a / the</u> last answer right.

5. **A:** Could you open <u>a / the</u> window, please?

   B: Which one?

   A: <u>A / The</u> one next to <u>a / the</u> door.

6. **A:** Who's that?

   B: That's <u>a / the</u> school principal.

   A: Oh, I've never seen her before.

7. **A:** Do you like <u>the / Ø</u> history?

   B: It's OK. But I prefer <u>the / Ø</u> science. What about you?

   A: I'm very interested in <u>a / the</u> history of <u>the / Ø</u> ancient Greece.

8. **A:** We learned about <u>an / the</u> ozone layer in science class yesterday.

   B: Did you know there's <u>an / the</u> enormous "hole" in it?

   A: Yeah. It's pretty scary.

   B: It sure is. It was <u>a / the</u> first time I'd heard about it.

9. **A:** What kind of work do you do?

   B: I'm <u>an / the</u> engineer. What about you?

   A: I'm <u>a / Ø</u> mechanic.

10. **A:** Are they <u>some / Ø</u> students?

    B: I don't think so. They look like <u>the / Ø</u> teachers.

11. **A:** Do you know where I can get <u>some / the</u> water around here?

    B: Sure. There's <u>a / the</u> water fountain right across <u>a / the</u> hall, right next to <u>the / Ø</u> rest rooms.

12. **A:** Do you know what <u>a / the</u> homework is for tomorrow?

    B: We have to read <u>a / the</u> fable.

    A: Which one?

    B: <u>A / The</u> one on page 23.

EXERCISE 2: Indefinite and Definite Articles

*Complete the conversation. Use **a, an,** or **the** where necessary. Leave a blank if you don't need an article.*

BING YANG: Hi, Georgina. What are you doing?

GEORGINA: I'm reading ____*a*____ fable for my English class.
                      1.

BING YANG: What's _____ fable? I've never heard _____ word before.
                      2.   **3.**

GEORGINA: _____ fable is _____ short story about _____ animals.
               4.   **5.**   **6.**

BING YANG: About _____ animals? Like _____ science story?
                      7.   **8.**

GEORGINA: No. It's _____ fiction. _____ animals act like _____ people. They usually
                      9.   **10.**   **11.**

   teach _____ lesson. _____ lesson is called _____ moral of _____
         12.   **13.**   **14.**   **15.**

   story, and it always comes at _____ end.
                                  16.

BING YANG: That's interesting. Who's _____ author of _____ fable you're reading?
                                      17.   **18.**

GEORGINA: Aesop. He was _____ ancient Greek writer.
                            19.

BING YANG: Oh, now I know what you're talking about. He's very famous. My parents used to

   read _____ fables to me when I was _____ child.
        20.   **21.**

GEORGINA: Well, they're also good for _____ adults. I'll lend you _____ book when I'm
                                         22.   **23.**

   finished if you're interested.

BING YANG: Thanks. I am.

*Complete this version of a famous Aesop fable. Use **a, an,** or **the** where necessary. Leave a blank if you don't need an article.*

The Fox and the Goat

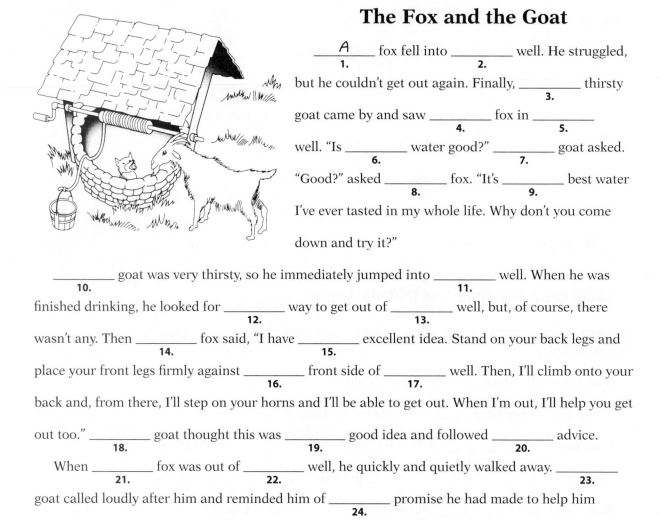

____A____ fox fell into _____ well. He struggled,
    1.   **2.**

but he couldn't get out again. Finally, _____ thirsty
                                            3.

goat came by and saw _____ fox in _____
                        4.   **5.**

well. "Is _____ water good?" _____ goat asked.
            6.   **7.**

"Good?" asked _____ fox. "It's _____ best water
                8.   **9.**

I've ever tasted in my whole life. Why don't you come

down and try it?"

_____ goat was very thirsty, so he immediately jumped into _____ well. When he was
    10.   **11.**

finished drinking, he looked for _____ way to get out of _____ well, but, of course, there
                                    12.   **13.**

wasn't any. Then _____ fox said, "I have _____ excellent idea. Stand on your back legs and
                    14.   **15.**

place your front legs firmly against _____ front side of _____ well. Then, I'll climb onto your
                                        16.   **17.**

back and, from there, I'll step on your horns and I'll be able to get out. When I'm out, I'll help you get

out too." _____ goat thought this was _____ good idea and followed _____ advice.
            18.   **19.**   **20.**

When _____ fox was out of _____ well, he quickly and quietly walked away. _____
        21.   **22.**   **23.**

goat called loudly after him and reminded him of _____ promise he had made to help him
                                                    24.

out. But _____ fox turned and said, "You should have as much sense in your head as you have
            25.

_____ hairs in your beard. You jumped into _____ well before making sure you could get
    26.   **27.**

out again."

MORAL: *Look before you leap.*

Complete the student's essay. There are twelve mistakes in the use of articles. The first mistake is already corrected. Find and correct eleven more.

THE FOX

                    a
A fox is ~~the~~ member of the dog family. It looks like the small, thin dog with an bushy tail, a long nose, and pointed ears. You can find the foxes in most parts of a world. Animal moves very fast, and it is the very good hunter. It eats mostly mice, but it also eats the birds, insects, rabbits, and fruit.

Unfortunately, a people hunt foxes for their beautiful fur. They also hunt them for another reason. The fox is a intelligent, clever animal, and this makes it hard to catch. As a result, the hunters find it exciting to try to catch one. It is also because of its cleverness that a fox often appears in fables, such as a fable we just read in class.

EXERCISE 5: Personal Writing

Write one or two paragraphs about the fable in Exercise 3 on page 108. Did you like it? Why or why not? What is the meaning of the moral? Give an example of the importance of the moral in your own life. Use some of the phrases from the box.

I once had an experience . . .	The experience taught me . . .
I think it means . . .	The fable is about . . .
I think the fable is very . . .	The moral of the fable is . . .

EXAMPLE: *I just read the fable called "The Fox and the Goat." The fable is about a fox that . . .*

_____

_____

_____

_____

_____

_____

_____

_____

_____

_____

_____

UNIT 19 Adjectives and Adverbs

EXERCISE 1: Spelling

Write the adjectives and adverbs.

Adjectives	Adverbs
1. quick	*quickly*
2. _____	nicely
3. fast	_____
4. good	_____
5. _____	dangerously
6. beautiful	_____
7. _____	hard
8. safe	_____
9. _____	ideally
10. _____	happily
11. _____	suddenly
12. peaceful	_____
13. angry	_____
14. _____	conveniently
15. bad	_____
16. _____	thoughtfully
17. _____	hungrily
18. extreme	_____

EXERCISE 2: Word Order: Adjectives and Adverbs

Emily is telling her friend about her new apartment. Unscramble the words to complete the conversation.

ANNA: Congratulations! <u>*I heard about your new apartment*</u>.
1. (heard about / I / apartment / new / your)

EMILY: Thank you! _____!
2. (news / good / fast / travels)

ANNA: What's it like?

EMILY: _____,
3. (five / rooms / has / it / large)

_____,
4. (building / it's / large / a / very / in)

and _____.
5. (sunny / it's / very)

_____
6 . (really / we're / with it / satisfied)

ANNA: Well, it sounds ideal. How's the rent?

EMILY: _____.
7. (too / it's / bad / not)

ANNA: And what about the neighborhood?

EMILY: _____.
8. (seems / quiet / it / pretty)
The landlord is a bit of a problem, though. He's friendly and very charming, but

_____.
9. (he / very / speaks / loudly)

ANNA: How come?

EMILY: _____.
10. (well / doesn't / he / hear)

ANNA: I guess nothing's perfect. I know you were looking for a long time.

_____?
11. (it / decision / was / hard / a)

EMILY: No. Not really. We really liked the apartment a lot, and it's located near school.

Besides, _____.
12. (quickly / had to / we / decide)
There were a lot of other people interested in it.

ANNA: Oh, no! Look at the time! _____.
13. (I / leave / now / have to)

_____!
14. (luck / with / good / apartment / new / your)

EMILY: Thanks. See you soon.

EXERCISE 3: Adjective or Adverb

Emily sent an email to a friend. Complete the email with the correct form of the words in parentheses.

Hi, Lauren,

I'm _____*totally*_____ exhausted! James and I finished moving into our new apartment
    1. (total)
today. It was a lot of _____ work, but everything worked out _____
    2. (hard)   **3. (real)**
_____.
    4. (good)

The apartment looks very _____. It's _____ _____. The
    5. (nice)   **6. (extreme)**   **7. (comfortable)**
only problem is with the heat. I always feel _____. We'll have to speak to the
    8. (cold)
landlord about it. He seems _____ _____.
    9. (pretty)   **10. (friendly)**

People tell me that the neighborhood is very _____. That's _____
    11. (safe)   **12. (real)**
_____ because, as you know, I get home pretty _____ from work. I
    13. (important)   **14. (late)**
hate it when the streets are _____ _____ like they were in our old
    15. (complete)   **16. (empty)**
neighborhood.

Shopping is very _____ too. We can get to all the stores very _____.
    17. (good)   **18. (easy)**
The bus stop is located _____ the apartment, and all of the buses run
    19. (near)
_____. Everything is _____ and _____.
    20. (frequent)   **21. (nice)**   **22. (convenient)**

Why don't you come for a visit? It would be _____ to see you.
    23. (wonderful)

Love,

Emily

P.S. I almost _____ forgot to tell you! James got a _____ job as a
    24. (complete)   **25. (new)**
computer programmer. He feels _____ _____ about it, and that, of
    26. (real)   **27. (happy)**
course, makes me _____ too.
    28. (happy)

Emily and James like old movies. They are going to download a few from the Internet. Circle the correct adjective forms to complete these brief movie reviews.

At Home at the Movies

BILLY BUDD Based on Herman Melville's powerful and (**1.** fascinated / fascinating) novel, this well-acted, well-produced film will leave you (**2.** disturbed / disturbing).

THE BURNING There's nothing at all (**3.** entertained / entertaining) about this 1981 horror film that takes place in a summer camp. You'll be (**4.** disgusted / disgusting) by all the blood in this story of revenge.

CHARIOTS OF FIRE Made in England, this is an (**5.** inspired / inspiring) story about two Olympic runners. Wonderfully acted.

COMING HOME Jon Voight plays the role of a (**6.** paralyzed / paralyzing) war veteran in this (**7.** moved / moving) drama about the effects of war. Powerful.

THE COMPETITION Well-acted love story about two pianists who fall in love while competing for the top prize in a music competition. You'll be (**8.** moved / moving). Beautiful music.

FOLLOW ME QUIETLY An extraordinarily (**9.** frightened / frightening) thriller about a mentally (**10.** disturbed / disturbing) man who kills people when it rains. Not for the weak-hearted.

THE GRADUATE Director Mike Nichols won an Academy Award for this funny but (**11.** touched / touching) look at a young man trying to figure out his life after college.

THE GREEN WALL Mario Robles Godoy's photography is absolutely (**12.** astonished / astonishing) in this story of a young Peruvian family. In Spanish with English subtitles.

INVASION OF THE BODY SNATCHERS One of the most (**13.** frightened / frightening) science-fiction movies ever made. You won't be (**14.** bored / boring).

WEST SIDE STORY No matter how many times you see this classic musical, you will never be (**15.** disappointed / disappointing). The story, based on Shakespeare's *Romeo and Juliet*, is (**16.** touched / touching), and the music by Leonard Bernstein is delightful and (**17.** excited / exciting).

WILBUR AND ORVILLE: THE FIRST TO FLY This is an exceptionally (**18.** entertained / entertaining) biography of the two famous Wright brothers. Good for kids too. They'll learn a lot without ever being (**19.** bored / boring).

Complete the sentences with the correct order of the words in parentheses.

1. Last night we downloaded two _____*funny old movies*_____ starring Claudio Reggiano.
   (old / funny / movies)

2. He's a(n) _____.
   (handsome / actor / tall / Italian)

3. The movie looked great on my friend's _____.
   (new / TV / large)

4. My friend served some _____.
   (delicious / pizza / mushroom / fresh)

5. We ate it on her _____.
   (leather / comfortable / black / sofa)

6. She just moved into this _____ near the college.
   (nice / apartment / small / student)

7. It's in a _____.
   (residential / quiet / neighborhood)

8. I had a very _____.
   (evening / enjoyable / relaxing)

9. I would like to find a(n) _____ like hers.
   (small / comfortable / apartment / affordable)

Read the ad for an apartment. There are ten mistakes in the use of adjectives and adverbs.
The first one is already corrected. Find and correct nine more.

── FOR RENT ──

Charming
~~Charmingly~~, one-bedroom apartment in a residential peaceful neighborhood.

Convenient located near shopping, transportation, entertainment, and more.

- affordable rent

- all-new appliances

- French antique beautiful desk

- friendly neighbors

- clean and safely neighborhood

- closely to park

- quiet building

This great apartment is ideal for students, and it's immediate available.

Call 444–HOME for an appointment. You won't be disappointing! But act fastly!

This apartment amazing won't last long.

Read the apartment ad in Exercise 6. Does the apartment sound good to you? Why or why not? What features are important to you in a home? Write a paragraph. Use some of the adjectives and adverbs from the box.

beautiful	good	nice	residential
convenient	inexpensive	old	safe
extremely	large	quiet	terribly
friendly	modern	really	very

EXAMPLE: *The apartment in the ad sounds very good. I like the fact that it is located in a residential neighborhood. It's really important to me to live in a quiet building . . .*

_____

_____

_____

_____

_____

_____

_____

_____

_____

_____

UNIT 20 Adjectives: Comparisons with *As . . . as* and *Than*

EXERCISE 1: Spelling: Regular and Irregular Comparatives

Write the comparative forms of the adjectives.

Adjective	Comparative
1. amazing	*more amazing*
2. bad	
3. big	
4. careful	
5. cheap	
6. comfortable	
7. crowded	
8. delicious	
9. early	
10. expensive	
11. far	
12. fresh	
13. good	
14. hot	
15. noisy	
16. relaxed	
17. terrible	
18. traditional	
19. varied	
20. wet	

EXERCISE 2: Comparisons with As . . . as

Look at the information comparing two pizza restaurants. Complete the sentences with **just as . . . as** *or* **not as . . . as** *and the correct form of the words in parentheses.*

	PIZZA PALACE	JOE'S PIZZERIA
Year opened	2000	2000
Number of tables	40	20
Pizza size	12 inches	12 inches
Price of a cheese pizza	$8.00	$8.00
Choice of pizza toppings	15	7
Average waiting time for a table	10 minutes	5 minutes
Hours	noon–11:00 P.M. (7 days a week)	noon–8:00 P.M. (closed Mondays)
Atmosphere	★★	★
Service	★★	★★
Cleanliness	★★	★★
Food	★★	★★★

1. The Pizza Palace is _____ *just as old as* _____ Joe's Pizzeria.
     (old)

2. Joe's Pizzeria is _____ the Pizza Palace.
     (large)

3. A pizza from Joe's Pizzeria is _____ one from the Pizza Palace.
     (big)

4. The pizza at the Pizza Palace is _____ the pizza at Joe's Pizzeria.
     (expensive)

5. The choice of toppings at Joe's Pizzeria is _____ the choice at the
     (varied)

   Pizza Palace.

6. The waiting time at Joe's Pizzeria is _____ it is at the Pizza Palace.
     (long)

7. The hours at Joe's Pizzeria are _____ the hours at the Pizza Palace.
     (convenient)

8. Closing hour at Joe's Pizzeria is _____ it is at the Pizza Palace.
     (late)

9. The atmosphere at Joe's Pizzeria is _____ it is at the Pizza Palace.
     (nice)

10. The service at Joe's Pizzeria is _____ the service at the Pizza Palace.
     (good)

11. The pizza at the Pizza Palace is _____ it is at Joe's Pizzeria.
     (good)

12. Joe's Pizzeria is _____ the Pizza Palace.
     (clean)

EXERCISE 3: Comparatives with *Than*

These conversations took place at the Pizza Palace. Complete the conversations with the correct form of the adjectives in parentheses. Use **than** when necessary.

1. **A:** Wow, this place has gotten really popular!

   B: I know. It's even _____*more popular than*_____ Joe's Pizzeria.
   (popular)

2. **A:** I can't believe how long the line is!

   B: Maybe we should come for an _____ dinner next time.
   (early)

3. **A:** I prefer that table over there.

   B: Me too. It looks _____.
   (comfortable)

4. **A:** Let's order pizza number 7—with spinach, mushrooms, and tomatoes.

   B: OK. That sounds _____ the one with pepperoni and extra cheese.
   (healthy)

5. **A:** Mmm. This pizza is delicious. It's _____ the traditional kind.
   (interesting)

   B: It *is* good, but I still think the pizza at Joe's is even _____ the
   (good)

   pizza here. And Joe's ingredients always seem somewhat _____
   (fresh)

   to me. Anyhow, that's just my opinion.

6. **A:** Hey, is that Brian over there at that table?

   B: No. Brian is much _____ that guy.
   (tall)

7. **A:** It sure is noisy in here. It's probably _____ on weekends.
   (bad)

   B: But it's a lot _____ at Joe's! And the atmosphere is
   (quiet)

   _____ too.
   (relaxed)

8. **A:** It's already 8:00.

   B: Oh! I thought it was _____ that.
   (late)

9. **A:** Do you ever make pizza yourself?

   B: No. I buy it frozen. It's _____ just to pop it in the microwave.
   (fast)

10. **A:** I really should buy a microwave oven.

    B: You really should. It will make your life _____.
    (easy)

Look at the chart comparing two microwave ovens. Complete the sentences with the appropriate comparative form of the adjectives in parentheses and **than**. Also, fill in the blanks with the brand—**X** or **Y**.

Brand	Price	Size (cubic ft.)	Weight (lbs.)	Defrosting	Heating	Speed	Noise
X	$181	0.5	31	●	○	◑	○
Y	$147	0.6	36	◑	●	●	◑

1. Brand ____X____ is ___more expensive than___ Brand ____Y____.
   (expensive)

2. Brand _____ is _____ Brand _____.
   (cheap)

3. Brand _____ is _____ Brand _____.
   (large)

4. Brand _____ is _____ Brand _____.
   (small)

5. Brand _____ is _____ Brand _____.
   (heavy)

6. Brand _____ is _____ Brand _____.
   (light)

7. For defrosting food, Brand _____ is _____ Brand _____.
   (efficient)

8. For heating food, Brand _____ is _____ Brand _____.
   (effective)

9. Brand _____ is _____ Brand _____.
   (fast)

10. Brand _____ is _____ Brand _____.
    (slow)

11. Brand _____ is _____ Brand _____.
    (noisy)

12. Brand _____ is _____ Brand _____.
    (quiet)

13. In general, Brand _____ seems _____ Brand _____.
    (good)

14. In general, Brand _____ seems _____ Brand _____.
    (bad)

EXERCISE 5: Comparatives to Express Increase or Decrease

*Look at the chart. It shows some food trends (increases and decreases). Complete the statements about the trends. Use the comparative forms of the adjectives from the box to show an increase or a decrease, or a cause and effect. Use both **more** and **less**.*

| big | cheap | ~~expensive~~ | good | healthy | heavy | popular | varied |

	1995	2005	2010
1. cost of a slice of pizza	$	$$	$$$
2. cost of a microwave oven	$$$	$$	$
3. quality of frozen pizza	+	++	+++
4. restaurant portion size	+	++	+++
5. choice of pizza toppings	+	++	+++
6. popularity of fast food	+	++	+++
7. health quality of fast food	+++	++	+
8. weight of fast-food customers	+	++	+++

1. A slice of pizza is getting _____ *more and more expensive* _____.

2. A microwave oven is getting _____.

3. The quality of frozen pizza is getting _____.

4. The size of portions in restaurants is getting _____.

5. The choice of pizza toppings is getting _____.

6. Fast food is becoming _____.

7. It's also becoming _____.

8. Fast-food customers are becoming _____.

EXERCISE 6: Cause and Effect with Two Comparatives

Read the information. Write a similar sentence using two comparatives.

1. When the pizza is salty, I get thirsty.

   The saltier the pizza, the thirstier I get. _____

2. When the ingredients are fresh, the food is good.

   _____

(continued on next page)

3. When the restaurant is popular, the lines are long.

   _____

4. When the meal is enjoyable, the customers are satisfied.

   _____

5. When the selection is big, the customers are happy.

   _____

6. When it's late in the day, the servers get tired.

   _____

7. When the restaurant is crowded, the service is slow.

   _____

8. When the service is good, the tip is high.

   _____

EXERCISE 7: Editing

Read the journal entry. There are eight mistakes in the use of comparisons. The first one is already corrected. Find and correct seven more.

I just got home from the Pizza Palace. Wow! The pizza there just keeps getting ~~good~~ *better*
and better. And, of course, the better the food, the more long the lines, and the
crowdeder the restaurant! But I don't really mind. It's totally worth it. Tonight Ana and
I shared a pizza with spinach, mushrooms, and fresher tomatoes. It was much more
interesting as a traditional pizza with just tomato sauce and cheese. It's also healthier
than. And the ingredients were as fresh than you can find anywhere in the city.
(Although I usually think the pizza at Joe's Pizzeria is fresher.) It was so large that
we couldn't finish it, so I brought the rest home. Actually, I'm getting hungry again just
thinking about it. I think I'll pop a slice into the microwave and warm it up. It will
probably taste almost as better as it tasted at the Pizza Palace!

EXERCISE 8: Personal Writing

What is your opinion? Write a paragraph about two meals you have recently eaten. Compare the experiences. Where did you eat? What did you have? How did you like it? Use the comparative form of some of the adjectives from the box.

big	fast	healthy	noisy
expensive	good	interesting	relaxing

EXAMPLE: *Recently, I ate in the school cafeteria. It was better than I expected. I had a chicken sandwich and a cup of tomato soup. The food was a lot cheaper than the food at the corner restaurant, and many of the choices were much . . .*

_____

_____

_____

_____

_____

_____

_____

_____

_____

_____

_____

Adjectives: Superlatives

EXERCISE 1: Spelling: Regular and Irregular Superlatives

Write the superlative form of the adjectives.

Adjective	Superlative
1. amazing	*the most amazing*
2. bad	
3. big	
4. cute	
5. dynamic	
6. expensive	
7. far	
8. funny	
9. good	
10. happy	
11. hot	
12. important	
13. intelligent	
14. interesting	
15. low	
16. nice	
17. noisy	
18. practical	
19. warm	
20. wonderful	

EXERCISE 2: The Superlative

Look at the information comparing the subway systems in three cities. Complete the sentences with the superlative form of the adjectives in parentheses. Also, write the name of the correct city.

THREE NORTH AMERICAN SUBWAY SYSTEMS			
	Toronto	**New York City**	**Mexico City**
First opened	1954	1904	1969
Length (miles)	42.4	229	109.6
Number of riders (per year)	280 million	1.6 billion	1.4 billion
Cost of a single ride*	$2.94	$2.25	$0.24

*in U.S. dollars

1. _____New York City_____ has _____the oldest_____ subway system.
   (old)

2. _____ has _____ subway system.
   (new)

3. _____'s system is _____.
   (long)

4. _____'s system is _____.
   (short)

5. _____ system is in _____.
   (busy)

6. _____ has _____ number of riders.
   (low)

7. The subway in _____ is _____ to use.
   (expensive)

8. You can buy _____ single ticket in _____.
   (cheap)

Read the comments posted on an online subway message board. Complete the sentences with the superlative form of the correct adjectives from the boxes. Use **the -est** *or* **the most / the least**.

Track Talk

| beautiful   big   easy   new   ~~old~~ |

I just got back from London. Completed in 1863, the Tube (that's what they call their

subway) is _____the oldest_____ in the world, but it works just fine!
                      1.

Completed just a few years ago, Sheppard Subway is _____
                                                              2.

metro line in Toronto. I just rode it. Very nice!

IMHO (In my humble[1] opinion), the Moscow subway stations are without question

_____ in the world. They have some really nice features.
          3.

Statues, chandeliers, and artwork on the walls make them look more like museums than

stations! It's also one of _____ systems to use. There are plenty
                                          4.

of maps and signs in the stations so you don't get lost. As you can see, I'm one of

_____ fans of this great public transportation system!
          5.

| comfortable   convenient   cool   dangerous   fast   hot   interesting |

I just got back from a week's vacation in New York City. We had a great time and rode

the subway a lot. I have to say the subway seats are _____ I've
                                                              6.

ever experienced! They are so hard. I heard they used to be made of straw.[2] In any case,

it's _____ way to get around town—no traffic to slow you
          7.

down. It's summer, and all the trains are air-conditioned. Get ready for one of

---

[1] *humble:* not considering your ideas as important or as good as other people's
[2] *straw:* dried stems of wheat or similar plants

_____ rides you've ever been on. In contrast, the stations are
                    8.

among _____ I've ever been in. I'm sure the temperature was
                    9.

over 100 degrees. That said, New York has one of _____
                                                           10.

systems in the world. It's open 24 hours a day, 7 days a week, and you can go all over the

place—even to the beach! And I think it's _____ form of
                                                    11.

transportation to take. You see all kinds of people. It's a very multicultural experience.

Really fascinating. And this may really surprise you, but some people say it's one of

_____ subway systems because there are so many people on it.
            12.

You're almost never alone—even late at night. I guess there's safety in numbers!

crowded	dangerous	efficient	expensive	historic	quiet

The subway in Athens is probably _____ in the world. When
                                                13.

they were building the system, they found the remains of ancient roads, shops, and baths.

They've made these part of the system.

Tokyo has _____ subway in the world. At rush hour, there are
                    14.

so many people, special workers help push them onto the trains!

Driving in Paris? Don't even think about it! _____ way of
                                                           15.

getting around is the Metro. As in all big cities, you need to be careful and watch your

stuff. Rush hour is definitely _____ time to ride the subway
                                        16.

because there can be pickpockets "working" the trains.

I love the subway system in Mexico City. First of all, at just 3 pesos (about 25 cents), it's

_____ ride in town (actually, in the whole world!). And because
            17.

the train has rubber wheels, it's one of _____ rides too.
                                                    18.

Read the tourist's postcard. There are seven mistakes in the use of the superlative. The first mistake is already corrected. Find and correct six more.

Hola!

Greetings from Mexico City! With its mixture of the old and the new, this is one of the ~~interestingest~~ *most interesting* cities I 've ever visited. The people are among the friendlier in the world, and they have been very patient with my attempts to speak their language. Spanish is definitely one of a most beautiful languages, and I really want to take lessons when I get home. This has been the most hot summer in years, and I 'm looking forward to going to the beach next week. The air pollution is also the baddest I 've experienced, so I 'll be glad to be out of the city. By the way, we definitely did not need to rent a car. The most fast and convenientest way to get around is by subway.

See you soon.

L.

EXERCISE 5: Personal Writing

Write a paragraph about your city or country. What are some of the best things about it? The worst? Use the superlative form of some of the adjectives from the box.

affordable	clean	easy	interesting
bad	convenient	friendly	nice
beautiful	difficult	good	safe

EXAMPLE: *One of the best things about living here is the people. They are among the friendliest and most interesting people I've ever met . . .*

_____

_____

_____

_____

_____

_____

_____

_____

_____

_____

_____

_____

Adverbs: *As . . . as,* Comparatives, Superlatives

EXERCISE 1: Spelling: Regular and Irregular Comparative and Superlative Forms of Adverbs

Write the comparative and superlative forms of the adverbs.

Adverb	Comparative	Superlative
1. aggressively	*more aggressively*	*the most aggressively*
2. badly		
3. beautifully		
4. carefully		
5. consistently		
6. dangerously		
7. early		
8. effectively		
9. far		
10. fast		
11. frequently		
12. hard		
13. intensely		
14. little		
15. long		
16. much		
17. quickly		
18. slowly		
19. soon		
20. well		

Look at the track-and-field records for five athletes. Complete the statements with the words in parentheses and **(not) as . . . as**.

	100-METER RUN	HIGH JUMP	DISCUS THROW
Athlete A	12.0 sec.	1.8 m	37 m
Athlete B	14.0 sec.	1.6 m	39 m
Athlete C	13.5 sec.	1.9 m	38 m
Athlete D	14.0 sec.	1.9 m	39 m
Athlete E	15.0 sec.	2.0 m	40 m

1. Athlete B _____ *didn't run as fast as* _____ Athlete A.
   (run / fast)

2. Athlete B _____ Athlete D.
   (run / fast)

3. Athlete C _____ Athlete D.
   (jump / high)

4. Athlete A _____ Athlete E.
   (jump / high)

5. Athlete C _____ Athlete E.
   (throw the discus / far)

6. Athlete D _____ Athlete B.
   (throw the discus / far)

7. In general, Athlete B _____ Athlete D.
   (do / good)

8. In general, Athlete A _____ Athlete C.
   (compete / successful)

EXERCISE 3: The Comparative Form of Adverbs

Basketball players from two teams are talking about their last game. Complete their comments. Use the correct form of the words in parentheses. Use **than** when necessary.

GEORGE: The other team played well, but we played much _____ *better* _____. That's

1. (good)

why we won.

⊕ ⊕ ⊕ ⊕

JAMIL: We played _____ our opponents. We really deserved to win,

2. (hard)

and we did.

⊕ ⊕ ⊕ ⊕

(continued on next page)

ALEX: It wasn't a great game for me. I moved _____ usual because of

                                      3. (slow)

my bad ankle. In a few weeks, I should be able to run _____. I

                                                             4. (fast)

hope that'll help the team.

RICK: Our shooting was off today. We missed too many baskets. We need to shoot a lot

_____ if we want to win.

     5. (consistent)

LARRY: I was surprised by how well they played. They played _____

                                                     6. (aggressive)

they've played in a long time. We couldn't beat them.

ELVIN: I'm disappointed. We've really been playing a lot _____ our

                                                    7. (bad)

opponents this season. We have to try to concentrate _____ in

                                                   8. (good)

order to break this losing streak.

RANDY: Team spirit was very strong. We played a lot _____ together,

                                                   9. (effective)

and it paid off.

CARLOS: Of course I'm happy with the results. But if we want to keep it up, we have to practice

_____ and _____. I think we just got

         10. (intense)   **11. (frequent)**

lucky today.

Now write the names of the players under the correct team.

Winning Team   **Losing Team**

George _____   _____

_____   _____

_____   _____

_____   _____

EXERCISE 4: The Comparative and the Superlative of Adverbs

*Look at the chart in Exercise 2 on page 131. Complete the statements with the correct form of the words in parentheses. Use **than** when necessary. Then complete the statements with the letter of the correct athlete—**A, B, C, D,** or **E.***

1. Athlete B ran _____faster than_____ Athlete __E__, but Athlete __A__ ran
   (fast)
   _____the fastest_____ of all.
   (fast)

2. Athlete _____ ran _____. He ran _____ all
   (slow)   (slow)
   the other competitors.

3. Athlete A jumped _____ Athlete _____.
   (high)

4. Athlete _____ jumped _____ of all five athletes.
   (high)

5. Athletes B and D didn't throw the discus _____ Athlete _____.
   (far)

6. Athlete _____ threw the discus _____.
   (far)

7. Athlete _____ won in two categories. He performed _____.
   (good)

8. At 15 seconds, Athlete _____ scored _____ in the run, but he did
   (bad)
   _____ the other athletes in the rest of the events.
   (good)

EXERCISE 5: The Comparative of Adverbs to Express Change

Read about some athletes. Write a summary statement about each situation. Use the correct form of the words from the box.

accurate	dangerous	~~fast~~	graceful	long
bad	far	frequent	high	slow

1. Last month Lisa ran a mile in 12 minutes. This month she's running a mile in 8 minutes.

   SUMMARY: _She's running faster and faster._

2. Last month she ran three times a week. This month she's running every day.

   SUMMARY: _____

3. Last month Josh threw the ball 10 yards. This month he's throwing it 13 yards.

   SUMMARY: _____

(continued on next page)

4. Last month when Jennifer shot baskets, she got only five balls in. Now when she shoots baskets, she gets at least eight balls in.

SUMMARY: _____

5. Six months ago, Mike jumped 4½ feet. Now he's jumping almost 6 feet.

SUMMARY: _____

6. Matt used to run an 8-minute mile. These days he runs a 10-minute mile.

SUMMARY: _____

7. The ice-dancing team of Sonia and Boris used to score about 30 points for their program. These days they are scoring more than 40 points.

SUMMARY: _____

8. The basketball team used to practice two hours a day. Now they practice three.

SUMMARY: _____

9. Jason drives a race car. Last year he had two accidents. This year he's had five.

SUMMARY: _____

10. Last year the team felt good about their game. Now they feel terrible.

SUMMARY: _____

EXERCISE 6: Editing

Read Luisa's online exercise journal. There are seven mistakes in the use of adverbs. The first mistake is already corrected. Find and correct six more.

Tuesday, June 11

I just completed my run. I'm running much longer ~~that~~ *than* before.

Wednesday, June 12

Today I ran for 30 minutes without getting out of breath. I'm glad I decided to run more slow. The more slowly I run, the farthest I can go. I'm really seeing progress.

Thursday, June 13

Because I'm enjoying it, I run more and more frequent. And the more often I do it, the longer and farther I can go. I really believe that running helps me feel better more quick than other forms of exercise. I'm even sleeping better than before!

Friday, June 14

I'm thinking about running in the next marathon. I may not run as fast than younger runners, but I think I can run long and farther. We'll see!

EXERCISE 7: Personal Writing

Write a paragraph about your English skills. How are you speaking? Are you understanding what you hear? How is your reading? Writing? Use the adverb forms of the words from the box (or your own ideas).

accurate	fluent	hard
easy	frequent	quick
fast	good	slow

EXAMPLE: *I think my English skills are really improving. I'm speaking more fluently, and . . .*

_____

_____

_____

_____

_____

_____

_____

_____

_____

_____

UNIT 23 Gerunds: Subject and Object

EXERCISE 1: Gerunds as Subject and as Object

Complete the article from a health magazine. Use the gerund form of the verbs in parentheses.

KICK UP YOUR HEELS!

In recent years, _____dancing_____ has become a very popular
        1. (dance)

way to stay in shape. In addition to its health benefits, it also has

social advantages. "I really enjoy _____ out and
        2. (go)

_____ new people," says Diana Romero, a twenty-eight-year-old word
3. (meet)

processor. "_____ all day at a computer isn't healthy. After work I need to
        4. (sit)

move." And Diana isn't alone on the dance floor. Many people who dislike

_____, _____ weights, or _____ sit-ups are
  5. (run)   **6. (lift)**   **7. (do)**

swaying to the beat of the swing, salsa, and rumba.

   So, if you are looking for an enjoyable way to build muscles and friendships, consider

_____ a spin on one of the many studio dance floors that are opening up in
        8. (take)

cities across the country. "_____ can be fun," says Sandra Carrone, owner
          9. (exercise)

of Studio Two-Step. So, quit _____ time, grab a partner, and kick up your
           10. (waste)

heels!

EXERCISE 2: Gerunds as Subject and as Object

Look at the results of this questionnaire on four students' likes and dislikes. Then complete the sentences below with appropriate gerunds.

Key: + enjoy
      ✓ don't mind
      − dislike

	KATIE	RYAN	LUKE	ANA
Dance	+	+	+	+
Walk	+	+	✓	✓
Do sit-ups	−	−	−	−
Play tennis	+	−	+	✓
Run	−	+	+	+
Lift weights	−	✓	−	+
Swim	✓	+	−	✓
Ride a bike	+	+	✓	+

1. Ryan is the only one who dislikes _____*playing tennis*_____.

2. _____ is the group's favorite activity.

3. Half the people dislike _____.

4. Half the people enjoy _____ and _____.

5. Katie and Ana don't mind _____.

6. Ana is the only one who enjoys _____.

7. Luke doesn't mind _____ or _____.

8. _____ is the most disliked activity.

9. Luke is the only one who dislikes _____.

10. He also doesn't like _____ or _____.

11. Katie is the only one who doesn't like _____.

12. Katie and Luke really like _____, but Ryan dislikes it.

13. _____ is the group's second favorite activity.

14. Ryan doesn't mind _____.

Gerunds: Subject and Object   **137**

EXERCISE 3: Gerunds after Certain Verbs

Sandra Carrone is having a dance party at her studio. Complete the summary sentences with the appropriate verbs from the box and the gerund form of the verbs in parentheses.

admit	consider	dislike	keep	permit	regret
ban	deny	enjoy	mind	~~quit~~	suggest

1. **LUKE:** Would you like a cup of coffee?

   KATIE: No, thanks. I haven't had coffee in five years.

   SUMMARY: Katie _____*quit drinking*_____ coffee five years ago.
   (drink)

2. **OSCAR:** Oh, they're playing a tango. Would you like to dance?

   RIKA: No, thanks. It's not my favorite dance.

   SUMMARY: Rika _____ the tango.
   (do)

3. **ANA:** Do you often come to these dance parties?

   MARIA: Yes. It's a good opportunity to dance with a lot of different partners.

   SUMMARY: Maria _____ with different partners.
   (dance)

4. **LAURA:** I don't know how to do the cha-cha. Could you show me?

   BILL: OK. Just follow me.

   SUMMARY: Bill doesn't _____ Laura the cha-cha.
   (teach)

5. **KATIE:** This is a difficult dance. How did you learn it?

   LUKE: I practiced it over and over again.

   SUMMARY: Luke _____ the dance.
   (practice)

6. **VERA:** Ow. You stepped on my toe!

   LUIS: No, I didn't!

   SUMMARY: Luis _____ on Vera's toe.
   (step)

7. **BILL:** Are you going to take any more classes?

   LAURA: I'm not sure. I haven't decided yet. Maybe.

   SUMMARY: Laura is _____ more dance classes.
   (take)

8. **KATIE:** I really love dancing.

   LUKE: Me too. I'm sorry I didn't start years ago. It's a lot of fun.

   SUMMARY: Luke _____ dance lessons sooner.

(not begin)

9. **BILL:** Why don't we go out for coffee after class next week?

   LAURA: OK. I'd like that.

   SUMMARY: Bill _____ out after class.

(go)

10. **LUKE:** You look tired.

    LAURA: I *am* tired. I think this will be the last dance for me.

    SUMMARY: Laura _____ tired.

(feel)

11. **DAN:** Would you like a cigarette?

    INA: I don't smoke. Besides, it isn't permitted here.

    SUMMARY: The studio _____.

(smoke)

12. **DAN:** You can't smoke in the studio?

    INA: No. But you can smoke outside.

    SUMMARY: The studio _____ outside.

(smoke)

EXERCISE 4: Gerunds after Prepositions

Complete the conversations with the correct preposition and the gerund form of the verbs in parentheses.

1. **KYLE:** Where were you? It's 7:30!

   JOHN: I know. I apologize _____*for being*_____ late.

(be)

2. **EMMA:** Are you excited about your vacation?

   JUSTIN: Oh, yes. I'm really looking forward _____ a

(have)

   break. I need one.

3. **AUSTIN:** I'm trying to stop smoking, but it's so hard.

   NOAH: Don't give up. I'm sure you'll succeed _____.

(quit)

4. **RYAN:** What's wrong? You look upset.

   SASHA: I have a test tomorrow, and I'm worried _____ it.

(pass)

(continued on next page)

5. Cheng: Where's José?

Cole: He's still at work. He insisted _____ late and
    (stay)

_____ his report.
    (finish)

6. Kevin: I'm tired _____ home every night. Let's go out.
    (stay)

Amber: Good idea. I'm in favor _____ out more.
    (get)

7. Kayla: I hear the school cafeteria is going to get a salad bar.

Megan: That's great. I believe _____ healthy choices for
    (have)

lunch. It's important.

8. John: Do you approve _____ smoking outside the
    (permit)

school building?

Simon: Actually, I don't. I'm opposed _____ in public
    (smoke)

areas. They should prohibit it.

EXERCISE 5: Editing

Read the online survey about smoking. There are seven mistakes in the use of gerunds. The first one is already corrected. Find and correct six more.

Smoking Survey

Click on the statements you agree with.

                    banning
○ I'm in favor of ~~ban~~ smoking in all public places.

○ I think to smoke should be illegal in parks and at beaches.

○ I approve to having free programs that help people quit to smoke.

○ To advertise cigarettes in newspapers and magazines is alright.

○ Smoking cigarettes are a private decision, and the government should not

make laws against it.

○ If people enjoy to light up a cigarette, that is their right.

EXERCISE 6: Personal Writing

Look at the chart in Exercise 2 on page 137. How do you feel about the eight activities in the chart? Write a paragraph. Use some of the phrases from the box.

I can get tired of . . .	I really dislike . . .
I can't get excited about . . .	I sometimes look forward to . . .
I don't enjoy . . .	I would like to start . . .
I don't mind . . .	I'm not opposed to . . .
I enjoy . . .	I've never considered . . .

EXAMPLE: *I know exercise is important. I try to do some every day, but there are some things I like better than others. Dancing is my favorite activity. I enjoy . . .*

_____

_____

_____

_____

_____

_____

_____

_____

_____

_____

_____

EXERCISE 1: Infinitives after Certain Verbs

Read the exchange of letters in an advice column. Complete the letters with the correct form of the verbs in parentheses. Use the simple present, simple past, or future for the first verb.

Dear Annie,

I've known John for two years. We share a lot of similar interests, and until recently got along great. Last month, we _____decided to get_____ engaged. Since then, our relationship

1. (decide / get)
has been a nightmare. John criticizes me for every little thing. I _____ a marriage counselor, but John

2. (want / see)
_____ with me. Last night, he even

3. (refuse / go)
_____ the relationship if I mention the idea of counseling again.

4. (threaten / end)
I don't understand what's going on. I still love John, but I _____

5. (hesitate / take)
the next step. Can we solve our problems? What should I do?

ONE FOOT OUT THE DOOR

Dear One Foot Out the Door,

I've heard your story many times before. You're right to be concerned. Obviously, John
_____ afraid of getting married. As soon as you got engaged, he

6. (seem / be)
_____ distance by criticizing you. I agree that counseling is a good

7. (attempt / create)
idea if the two of you really _____ together. Maybe each of you

8. (intend / stay)
_____ to a counselor separately before going to one together. It's

9. (need / speak)
possible that John _____ alone to discuss some of his fears.

10. (agree / go)
ANNIE

Read the conversations between men and women in relationships. Complete the two summary statements for each conversation.

1. **SHE:** We need to focus on our relationship. I *really* think we should see a therapist.

    HE: Well, I'm not going to.

    SUMMARY: She urged *him to see a therapist.* _____

    He refused *to see a therapist.* _____

2. **HE:** Could you please do the dishes tonight?

    SHE: Sorry. I don't have time. Could *you* please do them?

    SUMMARY: He didn't want _____

    She wanted _____

3. **HE:** Don't forget to buy some milk.

    SHE: OK. I'll get some on the way home.

    SUMMARY: He reminded _____

    She agreed _____

4. **SHE:** Will you do me a favor? Could you drive me to my aunt's?

    HE: OK.

    SUMMARY: She asked _____

    He agreed _____

5. **SHE:** Would you like to have dinner at my place Friday night?

    HE: Um . . . I'm not sure. Um . . . I guess so.

    SUMMARY: She invited _____

    He hesitated _____

6. **SHE:** Will you give me your answer tomorrow?

    HE: Yes, I will. That's a promise.

    SUMMARY: She wants _____

    He promised _____

(continued on next page)

7.   **SHE:** Would you like me to cut your hair? It's really long.

     HE: Oh, OK.

    SUMMARY: She offered _____

                     He is going to allow _____

8.   **SHE:** It's 8:00. I thought you said you'd be home at 7:00.

     HE: No. I always get home at 8:00.

    SUMMARY: She expected _____

                     He expected _____

9.   **HE:** Why didn't you call me before you left the office?

     SHE: I was going to, but I forgot.

    SUMMARY: He wanted _____

                     She intended _____

10.   **SHE:** Let's see a movie Friday night.

     HE: OK, but could you pick one out?

    SUMMARY: She would like _____

                     He would like _____

11.   **HE:** I plan on asking my boss for a raise.

     SHE: Great idea. I think you definitely should do it.

    SUMMARY: He intends _____

                     She's encouraging _____

12.   **SHE:** I'd like to get some more stamps.

     HE: Oh, I'll stop at the post office on the way home.

    SUMMARY: She wants _____

                     He volunteered _____

EXERCISE 3: Editing

Read the journal entry. There are ten mistakes in the use of infinitives. The first mistake is already corrected. Find and correct nine more.

Annie answered my letter. I didn't expect ~~hearing~~ **to hear** back from her so soon! She agrees that seeing a counselor is a good idea for John and me, but she advised we to go to counseling separately at first. That idea never even occurred to me, but I think that it's a really excellent suggestion. I don't know if John will agree going, but I'm definitely going to ask him to think about it when I see him on Saturday. I attempted to introduce the topic last night, but he pretended to not hear me. (He's been doing that a lot lately. He seems to think if he ignores a question, I'll just forget about it!) I won't give up, though. I'm going to try to persuade he to go. I have no idea how to find a counselor, so if he agrees to go, I may ask Annie recommend some in our area. Obviously, I want finding someone really good.

I still believe in us as a couple. Our relationship deserves to have a chance, and I'm prepared give it one. But I want John feels the same way. After all, it takes more than one person to make a relationship. I really need to know that he's 100 percent committed to the relationship. I can be patient, but I can't afford waiting forever.

EXERCISE 4: Personal Writing

What do you expect from your friends? Write one or two paragraphs. Use some of the phrases from the box or ideas of your own.

I count on them . . .	I prefer (them) . . .
I don't expect them . . .	I really need (them) . . .
I expect my friends . . .	I would like (them) . . .

EXAMPLE: *Friends are really important to me. I expect my friends to always tell me the truth. When I have a problem, I count on them . . .*

_____

_____

_____

_____

_____

_____

_____

_____

_____

_____

_____

_____

EXERCISE 1: Infinitives of Purpose: Affirmative Statements

Look at the chart. Make sentences with the words in parentheses.

SOME FUNCTIONS OF MOBILE DEVICES			
	CELL PHONE	**SMART PHONE**	**PDA**
make calls	●	●	●
take pictures	●	●	
search online		●	
send email		●	
connect to the Internet	●	●	●
create a "To Do" list		●	●
store addresses	●	●	●
play music		●	
translate words		●	

NOTE: Technology changes fast, so it is possible that today you can use these devices to do a lot more things!

1. *You can use cell phones and smart phones to make calls.*
   (make calls)

2. _____
   (take pictures)

3. _____
   (search online)

4. _____
   (send email)

5. _____
   (connect to the Internet)

6. _____
   (create a "To Do" list)

7. _____
   (store addresses)

8. _____
   (play music)

9. _____
   (translate words)

EXERCISE 2: Infinitives of Purpose: Affirmative and Negative Statements

Combine these pairs of sentences. Use the infinitive of purpose.

1. Ned got a job at Edge Electronics. He needs to earn money for school.

   Ned got a job at Edge Electronics to earn money for school.

2. Ned never brings money to work. He doesn't want to buy a lot of stuff.

   Ned never brings money to work in order not to buy a lot of stuff.

3. He uses most of his salary. He has to pay his college tuition.

   _____

4. He really wants an MP3 player. He wants to download music from the Internet.

   _____

5. He's going to wait for a sale. Then he won't pay the full price.

   _____

6. A lot of people came into the store today. They looked at the new multipurpose devices.

   _____

7. They like talking to Ned. They want to get information about the devices.

   _____

8. Someone bought a GPS. He doesn't want to get lost.

   _____

9. Another person bought a tiny camcorder. She wants to bring it on vacation.

   _____

10. She used her credit card. She didn't want to pay right away.

   _____

11. Ned showed her how to use the camcorder. It can do a lot of things.

   _____

12. She'll use it as a camera. She'll take videos.

   _____

EXERCISE 3: Infinitives after Adjectives

Some people are talking at a mall. Complete the conversations with the verbs from the box and the infinitive of purpose.

| eat | find | have | ~~keep up~~ | leave | pay | take |

1. A: I need to go to Edge Electronics.

   B: How come?

   A: I've decided to get a new smart phone. It's important _____*to keep up*_____ with

     the latest technology!

2. A: I'd like to return this PDA.

   B: Do you have the receipt?

   A: No, I don't. I got it as a gift.

   B: Hmmm. I see that there's no price tag on it. I'm very sorry, but it's necessary

     _____ the receipt in order to return it.

3. A: Why don't you use your credit card?

   B: I know it's convenient _____ with a credit card, but I prefer to use

     cash for small purchases. Call me old-fashioned!

4. A: I'm hungry. How's the food court here?

   B: It's actually very nice _____ there. The food is pretty good and

     there's a great view of the capitol building.

5. A: That was a good lunch. I'm ready _____ now. What about you?

   B: Sure. I'm done shopping. Let's go.

6. A: Well, here's the escalator.

   B: It's faster _____ the elevator. And it's right over there.

7. A: Do you want to see a movie?

   B: OK. But we don't have a schedule with us.

   A: No problem! I have my smart phone. It's easy _____ a movie

     with it. Let's see what's playing around here.

EXERCISE 4: Infinitives after Adjectives and Adverbs + *Too* or *Enough*

Complete the conversations. Use the words in parentheses with the infinitive and **too** or **enough**.

1. A: Did you get a new smart phone at the mall?

   B: No. It was still _____*too expensive for me to get*_____.
                         (expensive / me / get)

2. A: Are you really that unhappy with the phone you have now?

   B: Not really. It's _____ most everything I need to do.
                              (good / me / do)
   I just would like it to have some more functions.

3. A: Do you want to go to a movie tonight?

   B: It's 10:00 already. It's _____.
                                        (late / go)

4. A: Maybe we can go tomorrow night.

   B: Sure, if we finish dinner _____ by 7:00.
                                           (fast / leave)

5. A: I have an idea. Why don't we combine a movie with a late-night dinner afterward?

   B: OK. That is, if I'm not _____ awake!
                                         (tired / stay)

6. A: Do you think I can call Alicia now?

   B: At 10:00? Sure. It's not _____.
                                          (late / call)

7. A: Do you have trouble understanding her on the phone?

   B: Who, Alicia? Not at all. She always speaks _____.
                                                          (clearly / me / understand)

8. A: Could you please turn on the air conditioner?

   B: The air conditioner? It's not _____ the air conditioner!
                                               (hot / need)

9. A: You're not drinking your tea. What's wrong with it?

   B: Nothing. It's just still _____.
                                          (hot / me / drink)

10. A: How does Dan like his new phone?

   B: He likes it, and it's _____.
                                      (easy / him / program)

EXERCISE 5: Editing

Read the text messages. There are eight mistakes in the use of the infinitive of purpose and infinitives after adjectives. The first mistake is already corrected. Find and correct seven more. Check spelling too!

MESSAGES

to remind
ANDREA (4:45 PM): Did you call Sara ~~for reminding~~ her about dinner tomorrow night?

ME (4:50 PM): It's to early to call now. Don't worry. I set my alarm in order no to forget.

ANDREA (5:30 PM): Will you be home enough early to help me with dinner?

ME (5:45 PM): Not sure. I have to stop at the hardware store too buy some more paint for the kitchen.

ANDREA (6:00 PM): Don't we still have paint?

ME (6:05 PM): Yes. But I want to make sure we have enough paint to finishes the job. It'll be a major improvement.

ANDREA (6:10 PM): OK. Would it be too hard to you to make another stop on the way home? I need some butter and eggs for baking the cake for tomorrow night. ☺

ME (6:15 PM): No problem. See you soon. XOXOX

SEND   MENU

EXERCISE 6: Personal Writing

Imagine you just got a new smart phone. What do you use it for? How do you like it? Write a paragraph. Use infinitives and some of the words from the box (or your own ideas).

convenient	expensive	good	(not) too
easy	fun	(not) enough	small

EXAMPLE: *I just got a new phone. I love it. It's small enough to fit inside my pocket and I use it to do many things besides talk. I use it . . .*

_____

_____

_____

_____

_____

_____

_____

_____

_____

_____

_____

EXERCISE 1: Gerund or Infinitive

*Read the notice about a support-group meeting for people who are afraid of flying.
Complete the sentences with the correct form—gerund or infinitive—of the verbs in
parentheses.*

Stuck on the ground? Don't wait! Get help now!

Are you afraid of _____*flying*_____ ? Stop _____ in fear!
　　　　　　　　　1. (fly)　　　　　　　**2. (live)**

_____ is the safest form of transportation, but many people are too anxious
3. (fly)

_____ on a plane.
4. (get)

Do *you* avoid _____ because you're afraid to leave the ground? Would you
　　　　　　　　5. (fly)

like _____ your fear?
　　　6. (get over)

Don't let your fear prevent you from _____ all the things that you want
　　　　　　　　　　　　　　　　　7. (do)

_____. You deserve _____ a life free of fear. So, don't put it off.
8. (do)　　　　　　　　　**9. (live)**

Decide _____ something about your problem NOW. Come to our monthly
　　　　10. (do)

support-group meetings.

The next meeting is at 7:00 P.M., Tuesday, March 3 at the Community Center. We look

forward to _____ you there.
　　　　11. (see)

And don't forget _____ our website at <u>www.flyaway.com</u> for some helpful
　　　　　　　　12. (visit)

tips on _____ yourself off the ground!
　　　13. (get)

EXERCISE 2: Gerund or Infinitive

These conversations take place at a support-group meeting for people who are afraid of flying. Complete the summary statements about the people. Use the correct verbs or expressions from the box and the gerund or infinitive form of the verbs in parentheses.

afford	be tired of	~~enjoy~~	intend	quit	remember
agree	believe in	forget	offer	refuse	stop

1. **JASON:** Have you ever been to one of these support-group meetings before?

    AMBER: Yes. I like meeting people with the same problem. You get a lot of useful tips.

    SUMMARY: Amber _____*enjoys meeting*_____ people with the same problem.
    (meet)

2. **ANDREA:** Why did you start coming to these meetings?

    HANK: My fear of flying prevents me from doing too many things. It's very discouraging, and I finally want to do something about it.

    SUMMARY: Hank _____ afraid of flying.
    (be)

3. **DYLAN:** Would you like a cup of coffee?

    SYLVIE: No, thanks. I gave up coffee. It makes me too anxious.

    SUMMARY: Sylvie _____ coffee.
    (drink)

4. **CARYN:** I think these meetings are really helpful. You can learn a lot when you talk to other people about your problems.

    PAULO: I agree.

    SUMMARY: Caryn _____ to other people about her problems.
    (talk)

5. **MARY:** Did you bring the travel guide?

    SARA: Oh, no. I left it at work.

    SUMMARY: Sara _____ the travel guide.
    (bring)

6. **AMANDA:** Did you tell Amy about tonight's meeting?

    JOSHUA: No, *you* told Amy about the meeting. I heard you do it.

    AMANDA: Really? Are you sure?

    SUMMARY: Amanda doesn't _____ Amy about the meeting.
    (tell)

7. **Tyler:** You're late. I was getting worried.

   Emily: I'm sorry. On the way over here, I noticed that I was almost out of gas. So I went to fill up the tank.

   summary: Emily _____ gas.
   (get)

8. **Katie:** I know your parents live in California. How do you get there?

   Mike: I take the train. It's a long trip, and I lose much too much time.

   summary: Mike can't _____ the time.
   (lose)

9. **Camille:** I was afraid to come to the meeting tonight.

   Vilma: Well, I just *won't* live in fear.

   summary: Vilma _____ in fear.
   (live)

10. **Erin:** Have you made your flight reservations yet?

   Luis: Not yet. But I'm definitely going to do it.

   summary: Luis _____ a reservation.
   (make)

11. **Rachel:** Do you think you could help us organize the next meeting?

   Justin: Sure. Just give me a task to do and I'll be glad to help.

   Rachel: We don't have a date yet, but I'll let you know.

   summary: Justin _____ with the next meeting.
   (help)

12. **Axel:** Would you like a ride home?

   Joanna: Thanks. That would be great.

   summary: Axel _____ Joanna home.
   (drive)

EXERCISE 3: Gerund or Infinitive

Rewrite the sentences. If the sentence uses the gerund, rewrite it with the infinitive. If the sentence uses the infinitive, rewrite it with the gerund.

1. It's important to talk about your problems.

   Talking about your problems is important.

2. Going to a support group is helpful.

   It's helpful to go to a support group.

(continued on next page)

3. Working together is useful.

_____

4. It's smart to be careful.

_____

5. It's not good to be anxious all the time.

_____

6. Flying isn't dangerous.

_____

7. Doing relaxation exercises is a good idea.

_____

8. Traveling is wonderful.

_____

EXERCISE 4: Editing

Read Hank's post to a fear of flying forum. There are ten mistakes in the use of gerunds and infinitives. The first mistake is already corrected. Find and correct nine more.

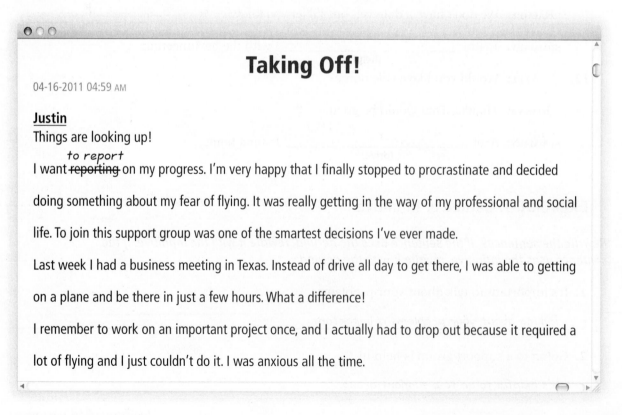

Taking Off!

04-16-2011 04:59 AM

Justin
Things are looking up!

    to report
I want ~~reporting~~ on my progress. I'm very happy that I finally stopped to procrastinate and decided

doing something about my fear of flying. It was really getting in the way of my professional and social

life. To join this support group was one of the smartest decisions I've ever made.

Last week I had a business meeting in Texas. Instead of drive all day to get there, I was able to getting

on a plane and be there in just a few hours. What a difference!

I remember to work on an important project once, and I actually had to drop out because it required a

lot of flying and I just couldn't do it. I was anxious all the time.

My fear was beginning to hurt my friendships too. I was dating a woman I liked a lot and we were

supposed to go on a trip. I canceled at the last minute because it required to take a plane.

Now I'm looking forward to do a lot of traveling. I know fear of flying is a universal problem, but it

doesn't have to be mine! It's a big world out there, and I plan on enjoy it.

EXERCISE 5: Personal Writing

Write a paragraph about a situation that makes you feel anxious or afraid. What do you do when you feel that way? Use some of the phrases from the box with gerunds or infinitives.

I always try . . .	I keep . . .	I try to remember . . .
I avoid . . .	I never quit . . .	It's important . . .
I imagine myself . . .	I often pretend . . .	Sometimes I can't help . . .

EXAMPLE: *I always get nervous before speaking in front of a group of people. As a result, I try to avoid getting into situations where I need to give a speech. When I can't avoid doing it, I . . .*

_____

_____

_____

_____

_____

_____

_____

_____

_____

_____

UNIT 27 Reflexive and Reciprocal Pronouns

EXERCISE 1: Reflexive Pronouns

Write the reflexive pronouns.

1. I _____ *myself* _____

2. my grandfather _____

3. the class _____

4. my aunt _____

5. you _____ OR _____

6. people _____

7. life _____

8. we _____

EXERCISE 2: Reflexive or Reciprocal Pronouns

Circle the correct pronouns to complete the sentences.

1. Anna and Jim phone (each other)/ themselves every weekend.

2. They have worked with each other / themselves for five years.

3. Anna herself / himself has been with the same company for ten years.

4. It's a nice place. All of the employees consider one another / themselves lucky to be there.

5. They respect each other / each other's opinions.

6. The boss herself / itself is very nice.

7. She tells her employees, "Don't push themselves / yourselves too hard!"

8. Anna enjoys the job herself / itself, but she especially likes her co-workers.

9. My brother and I are considering applying for jobs there myself / ourselves.

10. We talk to each other / ourselves about it when we jog together.

EXERCISE 3: Reflexive or Reciprocal Pronouns

Complete the conversations. Use reflexive or reciprocal pronouns.

1. **A:** What was Marianna's reaction when she lost her job?

   B: At first she was shocked. Then she told _____ *herself* _____ it's a chance to find

   a better job.

2. **A:** What do you do to maintain your relationship with the people you used to work with?

   B: We all live in different places now, but we call and email _____.

3. **A:** How does Miguel like his new job?

   B: Well, the job _____ isn't that interesting, but he really likes the

   people he works with.

4. **A:** So, you finally met Ina!

   B: Yes. I didn't realize that we had so much in common. We really enjoyed talking to

   _____.

5. **A:** Excuse me? I didn't hear what you just said. Could you please repeat it?

   B: Oh, it was nothing. I was just talking to _____! I do that

   from time to time.

6. **A:** Gina! Ricardo! Good to see you both. Come in and help _____

   to some food and drinks.

   B AND C: Thanks! We will. It looks great.

7. **A:** What happened to Frank's face?

   B: Oh, he cut _____ when he was shaving. It looks worse than it is.

8. **A:** You know, giving a party is a lot of work. Maybe we should think about this a little more.

   B: You're right. We need to ask _____ if we really have the time now.

9. **A:** How did you learn to play the guitar? Did you teach _____?

   B: No. A friend taught me.

10. **A:** Who are those two women over there?

    B: Oh, that's Olga and Marta. They just introduced _____ to me.

EXERCISE 4: Verbs with Reflexive or Reciprocal Pronouns

Gina had a party. Read each conversation and complete the summary. Use the correct form of the verbs in parentheses with an appropriate reflexive or reciprocal pronoun.

1. **JOYCE:** This party is a lot of fun.

   HANK: I've never danced with so any people in my life!

   SUMMARY: Joyce and Hank _____ *are enjoying themselves* _____.
   (enjoy)

2. **RON:** We were late because you forgot the address.

   MIA: It's not my fault. You never gave me the slip of paper!

   SUMMARY: Ron and Mia _____.
   (criticize)

3. **GINA:** I'm so glad you could come. There are food and drinks on that table over there.

   Why don't you take a plate and get some?

   CHEN: Thanks. I will. It all looks delicious.

   SUMMARY: Chen _____.
   (help)

4. **AMY:** OK, Amy. Now don't be shy. Go over and talk to that guy over there.

   TIM: Come on, Tim. You can do it. She's looking in your direction. Just go on over.

   SUMMARY: Amy and Tim _____.
   (talk)

5. **AMY:** Hi. I'm Amy.

   TIM: Hi. I'm Tim.

   SUMMARY: Amy and Tim _____.
   (introduce)

6. **AMY:** So, how do you know Gina?

   TIM: Oh, Gina and I were in the same class. What about you?

   SUMMARY: Amy and Tim _____.
   (talk)

7. **PAT:** Did you come with Doug?

   LAURA: No. Doug couldn't make it, but he let me use his car.

   SUMMARY: Laura _____.
   (drive)

8.   **Liz:** I'm sorry to hear about your job, Hank.

    Hank: It was my fault. I realize that I didn't take it seriously enough, but I've learned my lesson. It won't happen again.

    summary: Hank _____ .
                                       (blame)

9.   **Cara:** You know, I'm really glad we finally met.

    Liz: Me too. I feel like we've known each other a long time.

    summary: Cara and Liz _____ company.
                                       (enjoy)

10.   **Liz:** It was a wonderful party. Thanks for inviting me.

    Gina: Thanks for coming. And thank you for the lovely flowers.

    summary: Liz and Gina _____ .
                                       (thank)

EXERCISE 5: Editing

Read Liz's journal entry. There are eleven mistakes in the use of reflexive and reciprocal pronouns. The first mistake is already corrected. Find and correct ten more.

April 25

                myself

I really enjoyed ~~me~~ at Gina's party! Hank was there, and we talked to ourselves quite a bit. He's a little depressed about losing his job. The job himself wasn't that great, but the loss of income has really impacted his life. He's disappointed in himself. He thinks it's all his own fault, and he blames him for the whole thing. Hank introduced myself to several of his friends. I spoke a lot to this one woman, Cara. We have a lot of things in common, and after just an hour, we felt like we had known each other's forever. Cara himself is a computer programmer, just like me.

    At first I was nervous about going to the party alone. I sometimes feel a little uncomfortable when I'm in a social situation by oneself. But this time was different. Before I went, I kept telling myself to relax. My roommate too kept telling myself, "Don't be so hard on you! Just have fun!" That's what I advised Hank to do too. Before we left the party, Hank and I promised us to keep in touch. I hope to see him again soon.

EXERCISE 6: Personal Writing

Imagine you went to a party last weekend. Who did you go with? What did you do there? Who did you meet? What did you talk about? Did you have a good time? Write a paragraph about the party. Use some of the phrases from the box with reflexive or reciprocal pronouns.

dance	enjoy	introduce	see
drive	help	know	talk

EXAMPLE: *Last Friday night I went to a party by myself. I didn't know anyone there, but I introduced myself to some people. I met a very interesting . . .*

_____

_____

_____

_____

_____

_____

_____

_____

_____

_____

_____

EXERCISE 1: Particles

Complete the phrasal verbs with particles from the box. You will use some particles more than once.

| back | down | in | off | on | out | over | up |

Phrasal Verb **Definition**

1. call ___off___ *cancel*

2. call _____ *return a phone call*

3. come _____ *enter*

4. figure _____ *solve*

5. fill _____ *complete*

6. get _____ *return*

7. give _____ *quit*

8. go _____ *continue*

9. grow _____ *become an adult*

10. help _____ *assist*

11. look _____ *be careful*

12. point _____ *indicate*

13. take _____ *get control of*

14. take _____ *remove*

15. think _____ *consider*

16. turn _____ *reject*

17. turn _____ *start a machine*

18. work _____ *exercise*

EXERCISE 2: Phrasal Verbs

Complete the handout for Professor Cho's class. Use the correct phrasal verbs from the box.

do over	help out	look up	~~pick up~~	talk over
hand in	look over	pick out	set up	write up

Science 101   Instructions for Writing the Term Paper   **Prof. Cho**

1. _____*Pick up*_____ a list of topics from the science department secretary.

2. _____ a topic that interests you. (If you are having problems choosing a topic,
I'll be glad to _____ you _____.)

3. Go online. Use the Internet to _____ information on your chosen topic.

4. _____ an appointment with me to _____ your topic.

5. _____ your first draft.

6. _____ it _____ carefully. Check for accuracy of facts, spelling,
and grammar errors.

7. _____ your report _____ if necessary.

8. _____ it _____ by May 28.

EXERCISE 3: Phrasal Verbs and Object Pronouns

Complete the conversations between roommates. Use phrasal verbs and pronouns.

1. **A:** I haven't picked up the list of topics for our science paper yet.

   B: No problem. I'll _____*pick it up*_____ for you. I'm going to the science

   office this afternoon.

2. **A:** Hey, guys. We've really got to clean up the kitchen. It's a mess.

   B: It's my turn to _____. I'll do it after dinner.

3. **A:** Did you remember to call your mom back?

   B: Oops! I'll _____ tonight.

4. **A:** Hey, can you turn down that music? I'm trying to concentrate.

   B: Sorry. I'll _____ right away.

5. A: It's after 9:00. Do you think we should wake John up?

   B: Don't _____. He said he wanted to sleep late.

6. A: Professor Cho turned down my science topic.

   B: Really? Why did she _____?

7. A: When do we have to hand in our reports?

   B: We have to _____ by Friday.

8. A: I wanted to drop off my report this afternoon, but I'm not going to have time.

   B: I can _____ for you. I have an appointment with

   Professor Cho at noon.

EXERCISE 4: Word Order

Professor Cho made a list of things to do with her class. Unscramble the words to make sentences. In some cases, more than one answer is possible.

  1. the homework problems / back / give

    Give back the homework problems. OR *Give the homework problems back.*

  2. out / common mistakes / point

    _____

  3. them / over / talk

    _____

  4. a new problem / out / pick

    _____

  5. it / out / work / with the class

    _____

  6. up / the results / write

    _____

  7. go / to the next unit / on

    _____

  8. up / the final exam questions / make

    _____

(continued on next page)

9. them / out / hand

_____

10. study groups / up / set

_____

11. out / them / help

_____

12. Friday's class / off / call

_____

EXERCISE 5: Editing

Read the student's email. There are eleven mistakes in the use of phrasal verbs. The first mistake is already corrected. Find and correct ten more. A particle in the wrong place counts as one mistake.

Hi, Katy!

How are things going? I'm already into the second month of the spring semester, and I've got a lot of work to do. For science class, I have to write a term paper. The professor made ~~over~~ up a list of possible topics. After looking over them, I think I've picked one out. I'm going to write about chimpanzees and animal intelligence. I've already looked some information about them online up. I found up some very interesting facts.

Did you know that their hands look very much like their feet, and that they have fingernails and toenails? Their thumbs and big toes are "opposable." This makes it easy for them to pick things out with both their fingers and toes. Their arms are longer than their legs. This helps out them too, because they can reach fruit growing on thin branches that would not otherwise support their weight. Adult males weigh between 90 and 115 pounds, and they are about 4 feet high when they stand out.

Like humans, chimpanzees are very social. They travel in groups called "communities." Mothers bring out their chimps, who stay with them until about the age of seven. Even after the chimps grow up, there is still a lot of contact with other chimpanzees.

I could go on, but I need to stop writing now so I can clean out my room (it's a mess!) a little

before going to bed. It's late, and I have to get early up tomorrow morning for my 9:00 class.

Please let me know how you are. Or call me. I'm often out, but if you leave a message, I'll call

back you as soon as I can. It would be great to speak to you.

Best,

Tony

EXERCISE 6: Personal Writing

*How did you find out about this school? Write a paragraph about your experience choosing
the school and signing up for class. Use some of the phrasal verbs from the box.*

call up	find out	look up	talk over
figure out	help out	pick up	think over
fill out	look over	sign up	write down

EXAMPLE: *I found out about this school from my neighbor. She's been a student here for
several years, and she helped me fill out the forms . . .*

_____

_____

_____

_____

_____

_____

_____

_____

_____

_____

_____

UNIT 29 Necessity: *Have (got) to, Must, Don't have to, Must not, Can't*

EXERCISE 1: Affirmative and Negative Statements with *Must*

Read the driving rules. Complete the sentences with **must** *or* **must not** *and the verbs from the box.*

change	drive	~~have~~	leave	pass	stop	turn on
drink	forget	know	obey	sit	talk	wear

1. In almost all countries, you _____ *must have* _____ a valid license in order to drive.

2. You _____ a road test to get a license.

3. You _____ to carry your license with you at all times when you

   drive. Don't forget it!

4. You _____ all traffic signs. They are there for a reason!

5. When you see a stop sign, you _____. Don't just slow down.

6. You _____ faster than the maximum speed limit.

7. You _____ lanes without signaling.

8. When it's dark, you _____ your headlights.

9. You _____ the scene of an accident. Wait until the police arrive.

10. In most countries, the driver and passengers _____ seat belts.

11. In some places, you _____ on a cell phone unless you have a

    headset. Make sure you know the local laws.

12. Small children _____ in a special safety seat.

13. Alcohol and driving don't mix. You _____ absolutely never

    _____ and drive.

14. Driving regulations differ from country to country. You _____ the

    rules before you take to the road in a foreign country!

EXERCISE 2: Affirmative and Negative Statements with *Have to*

Read about driving rules in different countries. Complete the statements with the correct form of **have to** or **don't have to** and the verbs in parentheses.

	Minimum driving age	Maximum speed limit on major highway	Side of road	Seat belt law	Warning triangle	First-aid kit
Canada	16	62 mph/ 100 kmh*	right	driver and passengers	no	no
Germany	18	none	right	driver and passengers	yes (1)	yes
Indonesia	17	62 mph/ 100 kmh	left	driver and front seat passenger	no	no
Italy	18	81 mph/ 130 kmh	right	driver and passengers	yes (1)	recommended
Mexico	18	68 mph/ 110 kmh	right	driver and passengers	no	no
Turkey	18	74 mph/ 120 kmh	right	driver and passengers	yes (2)	yes

*depends on the part of the country

1. You _____*have to be*_____ eighteen years old to drive in most of the countries.
   (be)

2. You _____ eighteen in Canada and Indonesia.
   (be)

3. You _____ slower than 81 mph (130 kmh) in Turkey.
   (drive)

4. A driver _____ slower than 81 mph (130 kmh) in Germany.
   (go)

5. In Indonesia, drivers _____ on the left side of the road.
   (drive)

6. In Mexico, both the driver and passengers _____ a seat belt.
   (wear)

7. In Indonesia, backseat passengers _____ a seat belt.
   (use)

8. Turkish cars _____ two warning triangles to use in case they are
   (carry)

   involved in an accident.

9. In Germany, cars _____ two warning triangles.
   (have)

10. In Germany and Turkey, you _____ a first-aid kit in your car.
    (keep)

11. In Italy, you _____ one in your car.
    (have)

EXERCISE 3: Contrast: *Must not* or *Don't have to*

*Look at the chart in Exercise 2 on page 169. Complete the statements with **must not** or the correct form of **don't have to**.*

1. If you are under the age of eighteen, you _____ must not _____ drive in most of the countries listed in the chart.

2. You _____ be eighteen to drive in Canada.

3. You _____ obey a speed limit on major German highways.

4. In Turkey, you _____ drive on the left side of the road.

5. In Mexico, drivers _____ carry a warning triangle.

6. In Indonesia, passengers in the back seat _____ wear seat belts.

7. You _____ drive without a first-aid kit in Germany and Turkey.

8. You _____ have a first-aid kit in Italy.

EXERCISE 4: Statements, Questions, and Short Answers with *Have to*

*Complete the conversations with short answers or the correct form of **have to** (present, past, future, or present perfect) and the verbs in parentheses.*

1. **A:** Did you pass your road test the first time you took it?

   B: No. I _____ had to take _____ it two more times before I passed! What a hassle!
             (take)

2. **A:** _____ we _____ for gas?
                   (stop)

   B: _____. The tank's almost empty.

3. **A:** How many times _____ you _____ public
                   (use)

   transportation since you moved here?

   B: Only once. When my car broke down.

4. **A:** _____ you _____ late yesterday?
                   (work)

   B: _____. Luckily, I finished on time.

5. **A:** Are you thinking of buying a new car?

   B: Not yet. But in a couple of years, I _____ another one.
                   (get)

6. **A:** Why didn't you come to the meeting last night?

   B: I _____ my uncle to the airport.
          (drive)

7. A: My wife got a speeding ticket last week. She was really annoyed. She was only going five miles above the speed limit.

B: Really? How much _____ she _____?
(pay)

A: It was more than $100. They've gotten very strict about enforcing speed limits.

8. A: _____ your son ever _____ for a traffic violation?
(pay)

B: _____. He's a very careful driver.

9. A: _____ I _____ a new license when I move?
(get)

B: _____. You can only use an out-of-state license for 10 days.

10. A: Do you have car insurance?

B: Of course. Everyone in this country _____ car insurance.
(have)

11. A: How often _____ you _____ your car inspected in
(get)
your state?

B: Every two years.

EXERCISE 5: Contrast: *Must, Must not, Have to,* and *Can't*

Read the online test questions about road signs in the United States. Fill in the circle next to the correct answer.

---

1. When you see [YIELD] it means:

○ You must come to a complete stop.
○ You must not stop.
● You don't have to stop, but you must slow down and prepare to stop if necessary.

2. When you see [STOP] it means:

○ You don't have to stop.
○ You must stop.
○ You can't stop.

(continued on next page)

3. When you see SPEED LIMIT 50 it means:

- ⚪ You must drive 50 miles per hour.
- ⚪ You must not drive faster than 50 miles per hour.
- ⚪ You don't have to drive more than 50 miles per hour.

4. When you see NO TURN ON RED it means:

- ⚪ You have to turn when the light is red.
- ⚪ You don't have to turn when the light is red.
- ⚪ You must not turn when the light is red.

5. When you see DO NOT ENTER it means:

- ⚪ You must not enter.
- ⚪ You don't have to enter.
- ⚪ You must enter.

6. When you see DO NOT PASS it means:

- ⚪ You don't have to pass another car.
- ⚪ You can't pass another car.
- ⚪ You have to pass another car.

7. When you see ONE WAY ▶ it means:

- ⚪ You must drive in the direction of the arrow.
- ⚪ You must not drive in the direction of the arrow.
- ⚪ You don't have to drive in the direction of the arrow.

8. When you see MAXIMUM SPEED 65 / MINIMUM SPEED 45 it means:

- ⚪ You have to drive 45 miles per hour or slower.
- ⚪ You can't drive 70 miles per hour.
- ⚪ You don't have to drive 70 miles per hour.

9. When you see NO LEFT TURN it means:

- ⚪ You must turn left.
- ⚪ You can't turn left.
- ⚪ You don't have to turn right.

10. When you see ⓅNO PARKING 8:30AM TO 5:30PM it means:

- ⚪ You can't park at 5:00 A.M.
- ⚪ You must not park at 7:00 P.M.
- ⚪ You don't have to move your car at 6:00 P.M.

EXERCISE 6: Editing

Read the email. There are eight mistakes in expressing necessity. The first mistake is already corrected. Find and correct seven more.

Hi, Jason!

Sorry I haven't written before, but there are so many things I've ~~must~~ *had to* do since we moved

to California. For one, I have to taking a driving test. My brother is lucky. He must not

take one because he got a license when he was a student here. And you really have to

drive if you live here—it's very hard to get around without a car! So, I've been studying

the Driver Handbook, and I've found some pretty interesting—and sometimes

strange—things:

You can't smoke when a minor (that's someone under the age of eighteen) is in the car.

You can use a cell phone, but you has got to use one with a hands-free device.

You must no "dump or abandon animals on a highway." (I can't imagine anyone doing

this, can you?) If you do, you will probably must pay a fine of $1,000 or go to jail for six

months, or both!

Did you must take a road test when you moved to Italy?

I've got go now. Let me hear from you!

R.

EXERCISE 7: Personal Writing

Write a paragraph about a time you moved. What did you have to do? What didn't you have to do? Use some of ideas from the box and your own ideas.

buy furniture	learn to drive
find a place to live	make new friends
learn a new language	paint

EXAMPLE: *Moving is difficult. There are so many things you have to do. When I first came to this country, I stayed with my aunt and uncle. That was good because I didn't have to find an apartment right away. There were, however, many other things that I had to do. I had to . . .*

_____

_____

_____

_____

_____

_____

_____

_____

_____

_____

EXERCISE 1: Affirmative and Negative Statements with *Be supposed to*

Today, in some countries, when people get married, the groom's family often shares the expenses, and older couples often pay for their own weddings. However, some people are still traditional. Read the chart and complete the sentences with a form of **be supposed to**.

TRADITIONAL WEDDING ETIQUETTE: WHO DOES WHAT	
Role of the Bride's Family	**Role of the Groom's Family**
send invitations pay for food supply flowers pay for the groom's ring provide music	pay for the bride's ring give a rehearsal dinner[1] pay for the honeymoon provide beverages

[1] ***rehearsal dinner:*** a dinner that usually takes place the night before the wedding ceremony, attended by the bride, the groom, people who will be part of the ceremony, and often out-of-town guests

1. The groom's family _____*isn't supposed to send*_____ the invitations.

2. The bride's family _____ the invitations.

3. The bride's parents _____ the music.

4. The groom's parents _____ the music.

5. The groom's family _____ the groom's ring.

6. The groom's family _____ the bride's ring.

7. The bride's parents _____ the honeymoon.

8. The groom's family _____ the honeymoon.

9. The bride's parents _____ the rehearsal dinner.

10. The groom's parents _____ the rehearsal dinner.

11. The groom's family _____ the flowers.

12. The bride's family _____ the food.

13. The groom's family _____ the beverages.

*Erica Nelson is getting married. She completed this change-of-address form, but she made eight mistakes. Find the mistakes and write sentences with **was supposed to** and **wasn't supposed to**. Include the number of the item that has the mistake.*

U.S. Postal Sevice CHANGE OF ADDRESS ORDER	Customer Instructions: Complete Items 1 thru 9, Except Item 8, please PRINT all information including address on face of card.	OFFICIAL USE ONLY

1. Change of address for *(Check one)* ☑ Individual ☑ Entire Family ☐ Business

Zone/Route Id No.

2. Start Date Month `3 0` Day `0 6` Year `9 5`
3. If TEMPORARY address, print date to discontinue forwarding Month Day Year

Date Entered on Form 3982 M M D D Y Y

4. <u>Print</u> Last Name or Name of Business *(If more than one use, use separate Change of Address Order Form for each)*
`E R I C A`

Expiration Date M M D D Y Y

5. <u>Print</u> First Name of Head of Household (include Jr., Sr., etc.). Leave Blank if the Change of Address Order is for a business.
`N e l s o n`

Clerk/Carrier Endorsements

6. <u>Print</u> OLD mailing address, number and street *(if Puerto Rico, include urbanization zone)*
`2 6   M A P L E   R O A D`

Apt./Suite No. `4 A`   P.O. Box No.   R.R/HCR No.   Rural Box/HCR Box No.

City `B O S T O N`   State `M A`   Zip Code `—`

7. <u>Print</u> **NEW** Mailing address, number and street *(if Puerto Rico, include urbanization zone)*
`2 9 8 7   C O S B Y   A V E`

Apt./Suite No.   P.O. Box No.   R.R/HCR No.   Rural Box/HCR Box No.

City `A M H E R S T`   State   Zip Code `—`

8. Signature *(See conditions on reverse)*
Erica Nelson

OFFICIAL USE ONLY

9. Date Signed Month Day Year

OFFICIAL USE ONLY
Verification Endorsement

PS Form 3575, June 1991   ☆ U.S.G.P.O. 1992-309-315

1. Item ___1___   *She was supposed to check one box.*

OR

She wasn't supposed to check two boxes.

2. Item ____ _____

3. Item ____ _____

4. Item ____ _____

5. Item ____ _____

6. Item ____ _____

7. Item ____ _____

8. Item ____ _____

EXERCISE 3: Questions and Answers with *Be supposed to*

Erica and her new husband are on their honeymoon. Complete the conversations. Use the words from the box and **be supposed to.** *Use short answers when necessary.*

~~arrive~~	call	get	leave	shake
be	do	land	rain	tip

1. **ERICA:** What time ___are___ we ___supposed to arrive___ in Bermuda?

   ADAM: Well, the plane _____ at 10:30, but it looks like we're going to

   be late.

2. **ERICA:** What time _____ we _____ to the hotel?

   ADAM: Check-in time is 12:00.

3. **ERICA:** _____ we _____ if we're going to be late?

   ADAM: _____. We'd better call as soon as we land.

4. **ADAM:** How much _____ we _____ the person who carries our

   bags for us?

   ERICA: I think it's $1.00 a bag.

5. **ADAM:** _____ the hotel restaurant _____ good?

   ERICA: _____. The travel agent suggested that we go somewhere else

   for dinner.

6. **ERICA:** What _____ we _____ with our keys when we leave the

   hotel? Can we take them with us?

   ADAM: We _____ them at the front desk.

7. **ERICA:** _____ it _____ today?

   ADAM: No. _____. But look at those clouds. I think we'd better take

   an umbrella just in case.

8. **ERICA:** Can you hand me that bottle of sunblock?

   ADAM: Sure. _____ you _____ the bottle before you use it?

   ERICA: I don't know. What do the instructions say?

EXERCISE 4: Affirmative and Negative Statements with *Was / Were going to*

Read about Erica and Adam's plans. Write two sentences for each item. Use **was(n't)** *or* **were(n't) going to.**

1. Erica planned to be a doctor, but she became a lawyer instead.

   a. *Erica was going to be a doctor.*

   b. *She wasn't going to become a lawyer.*

2. Adam didn't plan to get married. He planned to stay single.

   a. _____

   b. _____

3. Erica and Adam planned to get married in June, but they got married in September.

   a. _____

   b. _____

4. They didn't plan to have a big wedding. They planned to have a small one.

   a. _____

   b. _____

5. Erica's sister was supposed to select the flowers, but Adam's assistant did it instead.

   a. _____

   b. _____

6. They wanted a short ceremony, but it was long.

   a. _____

   b. _____

7. They planned to live in Boston, but they moved to Amherst.

   a. _____

   b. _____

8. Adam didn't plan to change jobs. He planned to keep his old one.

   a. _____

   b. _____

EXERCISE 5: Editing

Read Erica's postcard. There are six mistakes in the use of **be supposed to** *and* **was** *or* **were going to.** *The first mistake is already corrected. Find and correct five more.*

Here we are in beautiful Bermuda. It's sunny, 80°, and it ~~will~~ 's supposed to get even warmer

later today.

    I'm so glad we decided to come here for our honeymoon. At first, we was going to go to

London, but we decided we really needed a relaxing beach vacation instead. The hotel is very

nice. We were supposed to get a standard double room, but when they found out we were on

our honeymoon, they upgraded us to a suite with an ocean view. Tonight we're eating at Chez

Marcel's. It supposes to be one of the best restaurants on the island.

    Gotta go now. I suppose to meet Adam in a few minutes. He's going to join me at the

beach, but decided to play some tennis instead.

    Thanks for offering to pick us up at the airport. We're supposed to arriving at 5:30 P.M.,

but check with the airport before to see if there are any delays. See you soon!

Love,

Erica

EXERCISE 6: Personal Writing

Everyone makes plans, but plans often change. Write a paragraph about your own changed plans. Use some of the phrases from the box.

> I was supposed to . . . , but . . .
>
> I wasn't supposed to . . . , but . . .
>
> I was going to . . . , but . . .
>
> I wasn't going to . . . , but . . .

EXAMPLE: *Three years ago I was supposed to move to California, but my plans changed. My father got a job in Texas, and so my family and I moved here instead. We were supposed to . . .*

_____

_____

_____

_____

_____

_____

_____

_____

_____

_____

_____

_____

Future Possibility: *May, Might, Could*

EXERCISE 1: Affirmative and Negative Statements

Read Lauren's journal entry. Complete the sentences with the words in parentheses.
Choose between affirmative and negative.

Thursday, July 3

I was supposed to go to the beach tomorrow, but the weather forecast says it

_____ might rain _____. I'm not really sure what I'll do if it rains. I think I
    1. (might / rain)

_____ shopping at the mall instead. It's a holiday weekend,
    2. (may / go)

so there _____ some good sales. I really need some new
    3. (could / be)

clothes. I _____ find a dress for John's party. Maybe I'll
    4. (might / be able to)

call Julie. She _____ to go with me. That would be great.
    5. (might / want)

She always knows the latest clothing trends.

On second thought, shopping _____ such a good idea.
    6. (may / be)

The stores will probably be really crowded. I _____ to a
    7. (could / go)

movie instead. There's a Spanish film at the local movie theater, but I'm a little afraid

that I _____ enough of it. My Spanish really isn't that
    8. (might / understand)

good. Maybe I'll call Eric and ask him if he wants to take a drive to see Aunt Marla

and Uncle Phil. He _____ to go, though, because he doesn't
    9. (might / want)

like driving in the rain. It's crazy how much the weather affects people's plans. Oh,

well. I _____ home and read a good book. That
    10. (could / stay)

_____ the best thing to do.
    11. (might / be)

EXERCISE 2: Contrast: *Be going to* or *Might*

*Read the conversations. Use **be going to** or **might** and the verbs from the box to complete the summary sentences.*

buy	go	rain	see	work
call	have	read	~~visit~~	write

1. **LAUREN:** Hello, Julie? This is Lauren. Do you want to go to the mall with me?

   JULIE: I don't know. I'm thinking about going to my parents'.

   SUMMARY: Julie _____*might visit*_____ her parents.

2. **JULIE:** What are you looking for at the mall?

   LAUREN: I need to get a new dress for John's party.

   JULIE: Good luck! I hope you find something.

   SUMMARY: Lauren _____ a new dress.

3. **LAUREN:** Do you think we'll get some rain?

   CARL: Definitely. Look at those clouds.

   SUMMARY: Carl thinks it _____.

4. **LAUREN:** What are you doing today?

   CARL: I have tickets for a play.

   SUMMARY: Carl _____ a play.

5. **LAUREN:** What are you doing this weekend?

   KAYLA: I'm not sure. I'm thinking about taking a drive to the country.

   SUMMARY: Kayla _____ for a ride.

6. **LAUREN:** Say, Eric. Do you want to see Aunt Marla and Uncle Phil tomorrow?

   ERIC: I can't. I have to go into the office this weekend—even though it's a holiday.

   SUMMARY: Eric _____ this weekend.

7. **LAUREN:** How about dinner Saturday night?

   ERIC: That's an idea. Can I call and let you know tomorrow?

   LAUREN: Sure.

   SUMMARY: Lauren and Eric _____ dinner together.

8. **LAUREN:** Hi, Aunt Marla. How are you?

   MARLA: Lauren! How are you? It's good to hear your voice. Listen, we just started dinner. Can I call you back?

   LAUREN: Sure.

   MARLA: OK. I'll speak to you later.

   SUMMARY: Marla _____ Lauren later.

9. **MARLA:** Hi. It's Aunt Marla. Sorry about before. What are you doing home on a holiday weekend? Why aren't you out?

   LAUREN: I'm tired. I just want to stay home with a good book.

   SUMMARY: Lauren _____ a book.

10. **MARLA:** Do you have any other plans?

   LAUREN: Maybe I'll catch up on some of my email.

   SUMMARY: Lauren _____ some email.

EXERCISE 3: Editing

Read Lauren's email. There are five mistakes in the use of modals to express future possibility. The first mistake is already corrected. Find and correct four more.

Hi, Rachel,

How are you? It's the Fourth of July, and it's raining really hard. They say it could ~~cleared~~ *clear* up later. Then again, it could not. You never know with the weather.

Do you remember my brother, Eric? He says hi. He might has dinner with me on Saturday night. We may go to a new Mexican restaurant that just opened in the mall.

I definitely might take some vacation time next month. Perhaps we could do something together. It might not be fun to do some traveling. What do you think? Let me know.

Lauren

EXERCISE 4: Personal Writing

A. *Make a short "To Do" list for next weekend. Put a question mark (?) next to the things you aren't sure you'll do.*

To Do

1.
2.
3.
4.
5.
6.
7.
8.

B. *Now write a paragraph about what you **are going to do** and what you **might do**.*

EXAMPLE: *I have a lot of plans for next weekend, but I know I won't be able to do everything. I'm definitely going to watch the football game with Tom and Lisa, but I might not have time to finish painting the kitchen . . .*

_____

_____

_____

_____

_____

_____

_____

_____

_____

_____

32 Conclusions: *Must, Have (got) to, May, Might, Could, Can't*

EXERCISE 1: Affirmative and Negative Statements with *Must*

Read the facts. Complete the conclusions with **must** *or* **must not**.

1. Jack is wearing a gold wedding band on his ring finger.

   CONCLUSION: He _____*must be*_____ married.
   (be)

2. You have been calling Alicia since 8:00 P.M., but no one answers the phone.

   CONCLUSION: She _____ home.
   (be)

3. Christa got 98 percent on her math test.

   CONCLUSION: Her parents _____ proud of her.
   (feel)

4. Carlos works from 9:00 to 5:00 and then attends night school.

   CONCLUSION: He _____ a lot of free time.
   (have)

5. Martin works as a mechanic in Al's Automobile Shop.

   CONCLUSION: He _____ a lot about cars.
   (know)

6. Monica owns two houses and four cars.

   CONCLUSION: She _____ a lot of money.
   (have)

7. Mr. Cantor always asks me to repeat what I say.

   CONCLUSION: He _____ well.
   (hear)

8. Chen got only four hours of sleep last night.

   CONCLUSION: He _____ very tired today.
   (feel)

9. Tyrone has been at R & L, Inc. for more than 20 years.

   CONCLUSION: He _____ a good position there.
   (have)

10. This job advertisement doesn't mention the salary.

    CONCLUSION: That's not a good sign. It _____ very good!
    (be)

11. Carmen was born in Mexico and moved to the United States when she was ten.

    CONCLUSION: She _____ Spanish.
    (speak)

(continued on next page)

12. Mindy never gets good grades.

CONCLUSION: She _____ enough.
                        (study)

13. Dan just bought a bottle of aspirin and four boxes of tissues.

CONCLUSION: He _____ a cold.
                       (have)

14. Ana and Giorgio didn't have any of the steak.

CONCLUSION: They _____ meat.
                         (eat)

15. Detective Menendez solves a lot of crimes.

CONCLUSION: His methods _____ very effective.
                                 (be)

EXERCISE 2: Contrast: *Must* or *May / Might / Could*

Read the conversations. Circle the appropriate words.

1. A: Someone broke into the Petersons' house.

  B: That's terrible! What did they take?

  A: All of Mrs. Peterson's jewelry.

  B: Oh, no. She could / ⟨must⟩ feel awful.

  A: Is she home now? I'd like to call her.

  B: I don't know. She might / must be home. She sometimes gets home by 6:00.

2. A: Do the Petersons have insurance?

  B: Oh, they could / must. Mr. Peterson works at an insurance company.

3. A: Have you checked our burglar alarm lately?

  B: Yes. And I just put in a new battery.

  A: Good. So it must / might be OK.

4. A: Do you remember that guy we saw outside the Petersons' home last week?

  B: Yes. Why? Do you think he might / must be the burglar?

  A: I don't know. I guess he must / could be the burglar. He looked a little suspicious.

  B: Maybe we should tell the police about him.

  A: Maybe.

5. A: Someone's at the door.

   B: Who <u>could / must</u> it be?

   A: I don't know.

   B: Detective Menendez wanted to ask us some questions about the burglary.

   A: Oh. It <u>must / could</u> be him. We're not expecting anybody else.

6. A: How old do you think Detective Menendez is?

   B: Well, he's been a detective for ten years. So he <u>must / might</u> be at least thirty-five.

   A: You're right. He <u>couldn't / might not</u> be much younger than thirty-five. He probably started

     out as a police officer and became a detective in his mid-twenties.

   B: He looks a lot younger, though.

EXERCISE 3: Short Answers with *Must* or *May, Might, Could*

Write a short answer to each question. Use **must, may, might,** *or* **could** *and include* **be**
where necessary.

1. A: Is Ron a reporter?

   B: _____*He might be*_____. He always carries a notepad and asks a lot of questions.

2. A: Does Marta speak Spanish?

   B: _____. She lived in Spain for four years.

3. A: Do the Taylors have a lot of money?

   B: _____. They're always taking very expensive vacations.

4. A: Is Ricardo married?

   B: _____. He wears a wedding ring.

5. A: Does Anna know Meng?

   B: _____. They both work for the same company, but it's very big.

6. A: Is your phone out of order?

   B: _____. It hasn't rung once today, and John always calls me by

     this time.

7. A: Is that online encyclopedia any good?

   B: _____. It's *very* popular.

(continued on next page)

8. A: Are Marcia and Scott married?

B: _____. They both have the same last name, but it's possible that

they're brother and sister.

9. A: Does Glenda drive?

B: _____. She owns a car.

10. A: Is Oscar an only child?

B: _____. I don't know. He's never mentioned a brother or sister.

11. A: Are the Hendersons away?

B: _____. I haven't seen them for a week, and there are no lights on

in their apartment.

EXERCISE 4: Contrast: *Might, Must, Could, Can't, Couldn't, Might not*

Read the description of a burglary suspect and look at the four pictures. Complete the conversation with the correct words and the names of the men in the pictures.

21-year-old white male

short, curly blond hair

no scars or other

distinguishing features

Allen

Bob

Chet

Dave

DETECTIVE: Please look at these four photos. It's possible that one of these men

_____ could _____ be the man we're looking for. Take your time.
    1. (must / could)

WITNESS 1: Hmmm. What do you think? _____ it be this man?
                                    2. (could / must)

WITNESS 2: It _____ be _____. He has a scar
                           3. (can't / must)   **4. (Name)**

        on his face. What about _____? He has short blond hair and
                                      5. (Name)

        looks like he's twenty-one.

WITNESS 1: I'm not sure. It _____ be. But it _____
                             6. (could / must)   **7. (might / must)**

        also be _____. He also has blond hair and looks twenty-one.
                          8. (Name)

WITNESS 2: But he has long hair.

WITNESS 1: The photo _____ be old. Maybe he cut it.
                              9. (could / couldn't)

WITNESS 2: That's true. Well, it definitely _____ be
                                 10. (couldn't / might not)

        _____. He looks too old. Maybe we could look at some
                11. (Name)

        more photos.

EXERCISE 5: Editing

Read the man's email. There are five mistakes in the use of modals to express conclusions.
The first mistake is already corrected. Find and correct four more.

                                             must

Just got home. It's really cold outside. The temperature ~~could~~ be below freezing because the

walkway is all covered with ice. What a day! We went down to the police station to look at

photos. I was amazed. They must having hundreds of photos. They kept showing us more and

more. We kept looking, but it was difficult to be sure. After all, we only saw the burglar for a few

seconds. They've got to have other witnesses besides us! There were a lot of people at the mall

that day. We may not be the only ones who got a look at the burglar! That's the one thing I'm

certain of! In spite of our uncertainty with the photos, the detective was very patient. I guess he

must be used to witnesses like us. Nevertheless, it have to be frustrating for him. I know the

police may really want to catch this guy!

EXERCISE 6: Personal Writing

Read the description of the burglar in Exercise 4 on page 188. Look at the pictures. Is one of them the burglar? What's your opinion? Write a paragraph. Use **could be, might be, may be, couldn't be,** *and* **can't be.** *Give reasons for your opinions.*

Ed

Frank

George

EXAMPLE: *It isn't always easy to identify someone. Is one of these men the burglar? It couldn't be . . . because . . .*

_____

_____

_____

_____

_____

_____

_____

_____

_____

_____

_____

WORKBOOK ANSWER KEY

In this answer key, where the contracted form is given, the full form is often also correct, and where the full form is given, the contracted form is often also correct.

UNIT 1 (pages 1–9)

EXERCISE 1

2. coming, comes
3. doing, does
4. getting, gets
5. going, goes
6. having, has
7. living, lives
8. looking, looks
9. meeting, meets
10. planning, plans
11. playing, plays
12. reading, reads
13. running, runs
14. saying, says
15. starting, starts
16. studying, studies
17. taking, takes
18. watching, watches
19. working, works
20. writing, writes

EXERCISE 2

2. is walking
3. isn't wearing
4. doesn't look
5. likes
6. doesn't understand
7. is
8. 's looking
9. 's getting
10. thinks
11. is
12. come
13. act

EXERCISE 3

Postcard A
2. 'm standing
3. is getting
4. looks
5. rains
6. has
7. 's taking
8. 's starting

Postcard B
1. love
2. 'm studying
3. living
4. is improving
5. speak
6. means
7. 're helping
8. want
9. miss

EXERCISE 4

3. Aldo and Emilia (OR They) go to school.
4. Aldo and Emilia (OR They) are having lunch.
5. Aldo works at the bookstore. Emilia studies at the library.
6. Aldo plays soccer. Emilia plays basketball.
7. Aldo is going home. Emilia is doing homework at the library.
8. Aldo has dinner. Emilia practices the guitar.
9. Aldo does homework. Emilia has dinner.
10. Aldo is playing computer games. Emilia is watching TV.

EXERCISE 5

2. Aldo doesn't watch TV. He reads the newspaper.
3. Emilia doesn't work at the bookstore. Aldo works at the bookstore. (OR She studies at the library.)
4. Emilia isn't playing tennis. She's playing basketball.
5. They don't always have dinner together. Aldo has dinner at 6:00. Emilia has dinner at 7:00.

EXERCISE 6

2. **A:** When do Aldo and Emilia get up?
   B: They get up at 7:30.
3. **A:** Does Emilia walk in the morning?
   B: No, she doesn't.
4. **A:** What are they doing now?
   B: They're having lunch.
5. **A:** Is Aldo doing homework now?
   B: No, he isn't.
6. **A:** Does Emilia do her homework at school?
   B: No, she doesn't.
7. **A:** When does Emilia play basketball?
   B: (She plays basketball) at 4:00.
8. **A:** Does Aldo play computer games before dinner?
   B: No, he doesn't.

EXERCISE 7

2. Emilia is usually on time.
3. Aldo and Emilia never miss school.
4. These days they're studying English. OR They're studying English these days.
5. They usually speak Italian.
6. Now they're speaking English. OR They're speaking English now.
7. Aldo and Emilia always do their homework.
8. Aldo is often tired.
9. The students usually eat lunch in school. OR Usually the students eat lunch in school.
10. They're always hungry.
11. At the moment, Emilia is having a snack. OR Emilia is having a snack at the moment.
12. Emilia rarely goes to bed late.

EXERCISE 8

How are you? ~~I write~~ *I'm writing* you this email before my class.

~~I'm having~~ *have* a part-time job as a clerk in the mailroom of a small company. The pay isn't good, but ~~I'm liking~~ *I like* the people there. They're all friendly, and we ~~are speaking~~ *speak* Spanish all the time. I'm also taking classes at night school. I'm studying the language and culture of this country. The class ~~is meeting~~ *meets* three times a week. It just started last week, so ~~I'm not knowing~~ *I don't know* many of the other students yet. They seem nice, though.

~~I'm thinking~~ *I think* that I'm beginning to get accustomed to living here. At first I experienced some "culture shock." I understand that this is quite normal. But these days ~~I meet~~ *I'm meeting* more and more people because of my job and my class, so I'm feeling more connected to things. I'm also having fewer misunderstandings because of the language.

What ~~do you do~~ *are you doing* these days? ~~Do you still look~~ *Are you still looking* for a new job?

Please write when you can. ~~I'm always liking~~ *I always like* to hear from you.

EXERCISE 9

Answers will vary.

UNIT 2 (pages 10–17)

EXERCISE 1

2. began	17. met
3. bought	18. moved
4. caught	19. needed
5. came	20. opened
6. died	21. put
7. did	22. read
8. felt	23. said
9. found	24. saw
10. got	25. took
11. gave	26. thought
12. had	27. understood
13. hurried	28. voted
14. kissed	29. won
15. lived	30. wrote
16. looked	31. was, were

EXERCISE 2

2. was	7. was, wasn't
3. weren't, were	8. wasn't, was
4. wasn't	9. were
5. was	10. were
6. wasn't, was	

EXERCISE 3

2. **A:** Where was Simone de Beauvoir from?
   B: She was from France.
3. **A:** What nationality was Pablo Neruda?
   B: He was Chilean.
4. **A:** Who was Wang Wei?
   B: He was a (Chinese) poet, musician, and painter.
5. **A:** Was Agatha Christie French?
   B: No, she wasn't.
6. **A:** What nationality was Lucy M. Montgomery?
   B: She was Canadian.
7. **A:** Was Nazim Hikmet a poet?
   B: Yes, he was.
8. **A:** When was Karel Čapek born?
   B: He was born in 1890.
9. **A:** Who was Isaak Babel?
   B: He was a (Russian) short-story writer and playwright.

EXERCISE 4

Biography A

2. grew up	5. loved	8. moved
3. taught	6. used	9. died
4. began	7. wrote	

Biography B

1. was	5. studied	9. had
2. planned	6. taught	10. died
3. began	7. loved	
4. painted	8. married	

Biography C

1. were	4. flew	6. took place
2. went	5. watched	7. lasted
3. built		

EXERCISE 5

2. **A:** Where did he grow up?
   B: He grew up in Hungary.
3. **A:** What did he do?
   B: He was a composer. OR He wrote music.
4. **A:** Did he spend his whole life in Hungary?
   B: No, he didn't.
5. **A:** Did Frida Kahlo plan to be a painter?
   B: No, she didn't.
6. **A:** When did she begin painting?
   B: She began painting after a serious accident.
7. **A:** What did she paint?
   B: She painted (pictures of) her family and friends. She also painted pictures of herself.

8. **A:** When did she die?
   B: She died in 1954.
9. **A:** Where did the Wright brothers build their first planes?
   B: (They built their first planes) in their bicycle shop in Ohio.
10. **A:** Did both brothers fly the *Flyer 1*?
    B: No, they didn't.
11. **A:** Where did the first controlled flight take place?
    B: (It took place) near Kitty Hawk, North Carolina.
12. **A:** How long did the flight last?
    B: (It lasted) only about 12 seconds.

EXERCISE 6

3. Orville didn't have serious health problems.
4. Wilbur didn't grow a moustache.
5. Orville didn't lose most of his hair.
6. Wilbur didn't take courses in Latin.
7. Wilbur didn't like to play jokes.
8. Wilbur didn't dress very fashionably.
9. Wilbur didn't play the guitar.
10. Orville didn't build the first glider.
11. Orville didn't make the first attempts to fly.
12. Orville didn't choose the location of Kitty Hawk.
13. Wilbur didn't have a lot of patience.
14. Wilbur didn't live a long life.

EXERCISE 7

    Pablo Neruda (1904–1973) ~~were~~ *was* a famous poet, political activist, and ambassador. He was born in Parral, Chile. His mother, a school teacher, ~~dies~~ *died* just two months after Neruda's birth. His father ~~work~~ *worked* for the railroad. He ~~no~~ *did not* support Neruda's early interest in writing. He wanted him to do something more "practical." When he was seventeen, Neruda ~~gone~~ *went* to Santiago to continue his education. At first, he planned to become a teacher like his mother, but soon he ~~beginned~~ *began* to write poems. He did not ~~finished~~ *finish* school, but he published his first book of poetry before he ~~were~~ *was* twenty. In one of his love poems he ~~describe~~ *described* "restless rocks" at the bottom of the ocean. Like the rocks in his poem, Neruda did not ~~stayed~~ *stay* in one place. He ~~spends~~ *spent* decades traveling and writing poetry. His poems ~~did show~~ *showed* strong emotions and beautiful imagery. In 1971, while he was Chile's ambassador to France, he ~~winned~~ *won* the Nobel Prize in literature. Neruda ~~dead~~ *died* two years later.

EXERCISE 8

Answers will vary.

UNIT 3 (pages 18–23)

EXERCISE 1

2. wasn't writing
3. was answering
4. were eating
5. weren't eating
6. weren't discussing
7. were discussing
8. wasn't answering
9. was returning
10. was attending

EXERCISE 2

2. **A:** What was he doing at 9:30?
   B: He was meeting with Ms. Jacobs.
3. **A:** Was Mr. Cotter writing police reports at 10:30?
   B: No, he wasn't.
4. **A:** What kind of reports was he writing?
   B: He was writing financial reports.
5. **A:** What was he doing at 11:30?
   B: He was answering correspondence.
6. **A:** Was he having lunch at 12:00?
   B: Yes, he was.
7. **A:** Who was eating lunch with him?
   B: Mr. Webb was eating lunch with him.
8. **A:** Where were they having lunch?
   B: They were having lunch at Sol's Café.
9. **A:** Who was he talking to at 3:30?
   B: He was talking to Alan.

EXERCISE 3

2. was crossing
3. was speeding
4. didn't stop
5. was
6. saw
7. was walking
8. saw
9. noticed
10. was going
11. reached
12. went
13. hit
14. took out
15. called
16. didn't stop
17. happened
18. came
19. got
20. was lying
21. was bleeding
22. was
23. were questioning
24. said
25. was crossing
26. went
27. knocked
28. happened
29. had
30. was crossing
31. didn't see
32. broke
33. had
34. were not

EXERCISE 4

2. What did you do when you heard the noise?
3. What did you see when you looked in the direction of the sound?
4. Where were you standing when you saw the Honda?
5. Did the driver stop when the accident occurred?
6. What happened next?
7. Did you get a look at the driver while he was driving away?
8. What was the victim doing when the car hit her?

EXERCISE 5

LONDON, June 31, 2009 Millvina Dean, the
last survivor of the 1912 *Titanic* disaster, ~~was dying~~ *died*
yesterday in Southampton, England. She was 97.

Dean had no memories of the disaster. She was
only two months old when she and her family were
passengers on the luxury ship's first voyage. The ship
~~sailed~~ *was sailing* from Dean's hometown of Southampton,
England, to New York City. On the night of April 14,
they ~~slept~~ *were sleeping* in their cabin when the ship hit a huge
iceberg. Dean's father became alarmed and
immediately sent his wife and two children to the
lifeboats. Dean ~~was believing~~ *believed* her father's quick
action saved their lives. Most people thought the ship
was unsinkable. "My father didn't take a chance," she
said.

Other passengers weren't as lucky. Just a few
hours after the *Titanic* struck the iceberg, the ship
~~was sinking~~ *sank* to the bottom of the Atlantic. More than
1500 passengers and crew lost their lives, including
Dean's father.

Dean's family returned to England, where she
spent most of her long life. In her later years, she
attended *Titanic* conferences and gave interviews.
She moved into a nursing home when she
~~was breaking~~ *broke* her hip three years ago. Charles Haas,
president of the Titanic International Society, said
that with Dean's death, history lost "the last living
link to the story" of the *Titanic*.

EXERCISE 6

Answers will vary.

UNIT 4 (pages 24–28)

EXERCISE 1

2. people used to read
3. people used to cook
4. people used to wash
5. people used to use
6. it used to take

EXERCISE 2

2. used to collect
3. didn't use to have
4. used to take
5. didn't use to be
6. used to live
7. didn't use to like
8. didn't use to know
9. used to return
10. used to make

EXERCISE 3

2. **A:** Where did she use to live?
   B: She used to live in New York.
3. **A:** Did she use to live in a house?
   B: No, she didn't.
4. **A:** What did she use to do?
   B: She used to be a student.
5. **A:** Which school did she use to attend?
   B: She used to attend City College.
6. **A:** Did she use to have long hair?
   B: Yes, she did.
7. **A:** Did she use to wear glasses?
   B: No, she didn't.
8. **A:** Did she use to be married?
   B: Yes, she did.

EXERCISE 4

2. would get up
3. would go
4. would not get
5. would have to
6. used to be
7. would get around
8. used to look
9. would fly

EXERCISE 5

Today I ran into an old classmate. We used to ~~was~~ *be*
in the same science class. In fact, we would often
study together for tests. He was a very good student,
and he always would ~~gets~~ *get* A's. At first, I almost didn't
recognize Jason! He looked so different. He
~~would have~~ *used to have* very dark hair. Now he's almost all gray.
He also used to ~~being~~ *be* a little heavy. Now he's quite
thin. And he was wearing a suit and tie! I couldn't
believe it. He never ~~use~~ *used* to dress that way. He only
used to ~~wore~~ *wear* jeans! His personality seemed different
too. He didn't use to talk very much. People didn't
dislike him, but he wasn't very popular. In fact, I

really ~~would~~ *used to* think he was a little weird. Now he seems very outgoing. I wonder what he thought of me! I'm sure I look and act different from the way I ~~was~~ used to too! I'm really glad we ran into each other. We shared a lot of the same memories. It was awesome! Maybe we'll see each other again!

EXERCISE 6

Answers will vary.

UNIT 5 (pages 29–33)

EXERCISE 1

2. Whose phone rang at midnight?
3. Who was calling for Michelle?
4. Who was having a party?
5. How many people left the party?
6. What surprised them?
7. Whose friend called the police?
8. How many police arrived?
9. What happened next?
10. Who told the police about a theft?
11. Whose jewelry disappeared?
12. How many necklaces vanished?

EXERCISE 2

2. How many rooms does her apartment have? (f)
3. How much rent does she pay? (j)
4. When does she pay the rent? (c)
5. Who does she live with? (h)
6. What does she do? (g)
7. Which company does she work for? (d)
8. How long does she plan to stay there? (a)
9. How does she get to work? (b)
10. Why does she take the bus? (i)

EXERCISE 3

2. Why did you leave Chicago?
3. Who moved with you?
4. Where did you get a job?
5. When did it start?
6. How many rooms does it have?
7. How many of the rooms came with carpeting?
8. How much do you each pay (a month)?
9. What do you need to buy?
10. Whose brother wants to visit her?
11. Who called last Sunday?
12. Who else did you speak to?
13. When do they want to visit you?
14. Why is there plenty of room?

EXERCISE 4

Why ~~the~~ *did* the defendant ~~had~~ *have* $10,000 in his wallet?
Who ^ gave him the money?
Why did the witness indicate Ms. Rivera?
Where did the defendant ~~met~~ *meet* Ms. Rivera?
Whose ~~Who~~ keys did he have? Were they Ms. Rivera's?
Which bus did Ms. Rivera take?
Why ~~she was~~ *was she* in a hurry?
Who ~~Whom~~ saw her on the bus?
What time did she get home?
Why ~~she did~~ *did she* look so frightened?
Who ~~she called~~ *did she call* when she got home?
What ~~did happen~~ *happened* next?

EXERCISE 5

Answers will vary.

UNIT 6 (pages 34–42)

EXERCISE 1

2. He isn't going to take the train.
   He's going to fly OR take a plane.
3. He isn't going to travel alone.
   He's going to travel with his wife.
4. They aren't going to leave from Chicago.
   They're going to leave from New York City.
5. They aren't going to fly US Airways.
   They're going to fly FairAir.
6. They aren't going to leave on July 11.
   They're going to leave on June 11.
7. They aren't going to take Flight 149.
   They're going to take Flight 194.
8. It isn't going to take off at 7:00 A.M.
   It's going to take off at 7:00 P.M.
9. They aren't going to sit apart.
   They're going to sit together.
10. She isn't going to sit in Seat 15B.
    She's going to sit in Seat 15C.

EXERCISE 2

2. How long are you going to stay?
3. Are you going to stay at a hotel?
4. What are you going to do in San Francisco?
5. Are you going to visit Fisherman's Wharf?
6. Is your daughter going to go with you?
7. What is he going to do?
8. When are you going to leave?

EXERCISE 3

2. will become
3. Will . . . replace
4. won't replace
5. will . . . operate
6. will . . . do
7. 'll be
8. 'll sing
9. 'll dance
10. Will . . . tell
11. will
12. won't . . . be
13. will . . . do
14. Will . . . have
15. will
16. will . . . help
17. 'll replace
18. 'll perform
19. won't be
20. will improve
21. will lose
22. will create
23. Will . . . need
24. will . . . look
25. won't look
26. 'll resemble
27. will . . . happen
28. 'll happen
29. 'll experience

EXERCISE 4

Next Wednesday is the first performance of *Robots* at Town Theater. Melissa Robins is playing the leading role. Robins, who lives in Italy and who is vacationing in Greece, is not available for an interview at this time. She is, however, appearing on Channel 8's *Theater Talk* sometime next month.

Although shows traditionally begin at 8:00 P.M., *Robots*, because of its length, starts half an hour earlier. Immediately following the opening-night performance, the company is having a reception in the theater lounge. *Robots* was a huge success in London, where all performances quickly sold out, but tickets are still available at Town Theater through March 28th. Call 555–6310 for more information.

EXERCISE 5

2. I'm going to do
3. I'll ask
4. it's going to rain
5. They're showing
6. we're going to have
7. it's going to spill, I'll be
8. I'll take
9. We're going to arrive
10. are we going to get
11. We'll take, will still be
12. We're landing
13. are you going to stay
14. we'll see

EXERCISE 6

2. 're seeing OR 're going to see
3. will . . . need OR are . . . going to need
4. starts
5. 'll get
6. are . . . going to eat OR are . . . eating
7. 're having OR 're going to have
8. are . . . getting OR are . . . going to get OR will . . . get

9. leaves
10. 's going to rain
11. 'll take
12. 'll lie OR 'm going to lie
13. 'll wake
14. is going to be OR will be

EXERCISE 7

I'm going
~~I going~~ to stay here for a week with my parents. Our hotel is incredible, and I spent the afternoon floating in the pool.

We have a lot of fun things planned. Tomorrow *we're seeing* OR *we're going to see* night ~~we'll see~~ a play called *Robots*. Mom already bought the tickets for it. The play begins at 7:30, and *we're having* OR *we're going to have* before that ~~we have~~ dinner on Fisherman's Wharf. Right now we're sitting in Golden Gate Park, but

's going to we have to leave. The sky is getting very dark. It ~~will~~ rain!

'll call
I ~~call~~ you soon.

EXERCISE 8

Answers will vary.

UNIT 7 (pages 43–47)

EXERCISE 1

2. gets up . . . 'll take (i)
3. is . . . 'll drink (c)
4. eat . . . 'll read (j)
5. finish . . . 'll do (g)
6. washes . . . 'll dry (e)
7. get in . . . 'll fasten (d)
8. gets . . . 'll drive (b)
9. stops . . . 'll need (f)
10. is . . . 'll be (a)

EXERCISE 2

2. will apply (OR 's going to apply) . . . before . . . finishes
3. After . . . finishes . . . 'll visit (OR 's going to visit)
4. While . . . works . . . 'll take (OR 's going to take)
5. 'll visit (OR 's going to visit) . . . before . . . gets
6. When . . . finishes . . . 'll fly (OR 's going to fly)
7. 'll attend (OR 's going to attend) . . . when . . . 's
8. 'll return (OR 's going to return) . . . after . . . attends
9. 'll move (OR 's going to move) . . . when . . . returns
10. After . . . moves . . . will look for (OR 's going to look for)

EXERCISE 3

2. . . . Vera saves enough money from her job, she's going to (OR she'll) buy a plane ticket.
3. . . . Vera goes home, she's going to buy presents for her family.
4. . . . Vera arrives at the airport, her father will be there to drive her home.
5. . . . Vera and her father get home, they'll have dinner.
6. Vera will give her family the presents . . . they finish dinner.
7. Vera's brother will wash the dishes . . . Vera's sister dries them.
8. The whole family is going to stay up talking . . . the clock strikes midnight.
9. . . . they go to bed, they'll all feel very tired.
10. Vera will fall asleep . . . her head hits the pillow.
11. . . . Vera wakes up the next morning, she's going to call her friends.
12. She'll see her friends . . . she has breakfast.

EXERCISE 4

I have a lot of goals, but I need to get more organized if I want to achieve them. So, tomorrow I'm going to start working on them. College is my number one goal. As soon as I ~~will~~ get up, I'm going to download some online college catalogs. After I
examine them carefully, I ^'ll OR 'm going to^ choose a few schools that
interest me and I ^'ll OR 'm going to^ try to set up some visits. Maybe I can even get some interviews with some teachers at
the school. When ~~I'm going~~ ^I go^ to visit the schools, I'll also try to speak to other students. That's always a
good way to find out about a place. After ~~I'm seeing~~ ^see^
several schools, I ^'ll OR 'm going to^ decide which ones to apply to. When I get accepted, I'll make the best choice. While
I'm in school, I'll study hard and in four years I ^'ll OR 'm going to^ have my degree!

EXERCISE 5

Answers will vary.

UNIT 8 (pages 48–53)

EXERCISE 1

2. broken
3. come
4. fallen
5. gone
6. had
7. lost
8. played
9. watched
10. won

EXERCISE 2

2. since
3. since
4. for
5. Since
6. For
7. for
8. since

EXERCISE 3

2. for
3. Since
4. has reached
5. Since
6. has gone on
7. has played
8. Since
9. has continued
10. has earned
11. For
12. has been
13. has been
14. since
15. has continued
16. since
17. Since
18. has broken
19. has . . . won
20. since
21. For
22. has had
23. has stopped
24. Since
25. 've dreamed

EXERCISE 4

2. **A:** How long has she had a record-breaking career?
   B: She has had a record-breaking career since she was ten OR since she became the youngest player to qualify for the USGA amateur championship.
3. **A:** How long has she been a professional golfer?
   B: (She has been a professional golfer) since she was sixteen. OR for _____ years.
4. **A:** Has she had any endorsement contracts?
   B: Yes, she has. (She has had endorsement contracts since she turned pro. OR since she was sixteen.)
5. **A:** How long has Juan Martin del Potro been a tennis player?
   B: (He has been a tennis player) since he was seven. OR for more than sixteen years.
6. **A:** How much money has he won since he turned pro?
   B: He has won millions of dollars (since he turned pro).
7. **A:** What kind of problems has he had for years?
   B: He has had a lot of physical problems (for years).
8. **A:** Has he won any titles since 2008?
   B: Yes, he has. (He won the U.S. Open.)

EXERCISE 5

3. Min Ho has won three awards
4. Marilyn has entered two competitions
5. Victor and Marilyn haven't seen each other since 2010.
6. Karl has been a tennis player since 2009.
7. Karl has lost three tournaments
8. Andreas hasn't been to (OR gone to) a tennis match

EXERCISE 6

What a great game! Marissa has been my favorite
for
~~since~~ years!

I heard that Taylor got $350,000 for winning
yesterday's tournament. How much money
has he made
~~does he make~~ since he turned pro? Does anyone
know?

Do you think Lee can support himself playing golf?
won
He hasn't ~~win~~ a major tournament for two years.
That's a long time!

hasn't won
Karla ~~didn't win~~ a game since last year. I really feel
bad for her.

Walter has stopped playing twice since January
because of injuries. That's really too bad.

I haven't had the opportunity to attend a competition
for
~~since~~ three years. This one is awesome!

I used to think golf was boring. Not anymore. I
haven't enjoyed
~~don't enjoy~~ a sports event so much for years!

improved
I think Juan's game has ~~improve~~ dramatically since
he won the last tournament.

has
Antonio's positive attitude ~~have~~ helped him improve
his game since he lost the match last month. I
consider him a role model.

EXERCISE 7

Answers will vary.

UNIT 9 (pages 54–58)

EXERCISE 1

2. become
3. chosen
4. cleaned
5. danced
6. drunk
7. fought
8. found
9. gotten
10. given
11. held
12. kept
13. known
14. looked
15. planned
16. sung
17. smiled
18. thrown

EXERCISE 2

4. 've
5. already
6. looked
7. still
8. haven't found
9. 've
10. already
11. seen
12. have not gone
13. yet
14. have
15. already
16. wasted
17. Have
18. decided
19. yet
20. haven't made up
21. yet

EXERCISE 3

3. Has she bought two bookcases yet? Yes, she's already bought two bookcases.
4. Has she thrown away old magazines yet? No, she hasn't thrown away old magazines yet. OR No, she hasn't yet thrown away old magazines. OR No, she still hasn't thrown away old magazines.
5. Has she found a professional painter yet? No, she hasn't found a professional painter yet. OR No, she hasn't yet found a professional painter. OR No, she still hasn't found a professional painter.
6. Has she collected boxes for packing yet? Yes, she's already collected boxes for packing.
7. Has she bought a new couch yet? No, she hasn't bought a new couch yet. OR No, she hasn't yet bought a new couch. OR No, she still hasn't bought a new couch.
8. Has she given away the old couch yet? Yes, she's already given away the old couch.
9. Has she cleaned the refrigerator and stove yet? No, she hasn't cleaned the refrigerator and stove yet. OR No, she hasn't yet cleaned the refrigerator and stove. OR No, she still hasn't cleaned the refrigerator and stove.
10. Has she made a list of cleaning supplies yet? Yes, she's already made a list of cleaning supplies.
11. Has she gotten a change-of-address form from the post office yet? Yes, she's already gotten a change-of-address form from the post office.
12. Has she invited the neighbors over for a good-bye party yet? No, she hasn't invited the neighbors over for a good-bye party yet. OR No, she hasn't yet invited the neighbors over for a good-bye party. OR No, she still hasn't invited the neighbors for a good-bye party.

EXERCISE 4

I'm writing to you from our new apartment! It
took us a long time to find, but finally, with some
professional advice, we were successful. We've

been
already ~~be~~ here two weeks, and we feel very much at home. But there's still a lot to do. Believe it or

*yet**
not, we haven't unpacked all the boxes ~~still~~! We took most of our old furniture, so we don't need to get too much new stuff. We had to buy a new couch for the

yet
living room, but they haven't delivered it ~~already~~.

met
We've already ~~meet~~ some of our new neighbors.

has
They seem very nice. One of them ~~have~~ already invited us over for coffee.

Have
~~Had~~ you made vacation plans yet? As soon as we get the couch (it's a sleeper), we'd love for you to visit.

We've already planned
~~Already we've planned~~ places to take you when you come, but let us know if there are specific things you'd like to do or see.

*OR . . . still haven't unpacked . . .

EXERCISE 5

Answers will vary.

UNIT 10 (pages 59–63)

EXERCISE 1

2. decided
3. flown
4. gone
5. heard
6. kept
7. made
8. ridden
9. seen
10. swum
11. traveled
12. worked

EXERCISE 2

2. 've ridden
3. 've heard
4. 've seen
5. 's flown
6. 've swum
7. has decided
8. 's worked

EXERCISE 3

2. have appeared
3. have . . . loved
4. have not stopped
5. has researched
6. (has) written
7. have . . . received
8. has described
9. has found
10. has promised
11. have not become
12. have increased
13. has continued
14. has . . . encouraged
15. have not read

EXERCISE 4

2. How many times have you visited, I've visited Europe more than 10 times.
3. Have you ever been, I've recently been on an African safari.

4. Have you ever been, Yes, I've been to Costa Rica.
5. How often have you been, I've been there once.
6. Have you (ever) traveled, No, I've never traveled in China.
7. Have you ever gone up, No, I've never gone up in a hot-air balloon.
8. Have you ever swum, I've swum with dolphins many times (OR six or more times).
9. Have you ever taken, No, I've never taken a group tour.

EXERCISE 5

ever been
Q: Have you ~~been ever~~ to Barcelona? I'm planning a trip there this summer and would love some tips.

A: I've never been there, but you can find a lot of useful information on websites such as tripadvisor.com.

returned
Q: I~~'ve returned~~ last week from a safari in Africa. It was awesome, and I'm really interested in sharing photos with other travelers. Any ideas?

A: Yes! We've recently formed an online discussion group on safaris and we post photos there. Contact me at travcal@oal.com for more information.

Q: I'm trying to choose a hotel for my trip to

stayed
Toronto. Has anyone you know ever ~~stays~~ at the Victoria?

stayed there several times
A: I've ~~several times stayed there~~ myself. It's convenient and affordable. I think you'd like it.

Q: I'm going to be traveling alone in the south of France. What's the best form of transportation for getting around? I can't afford to rent a car.

taken
A: I've always ~~took~~ local busses. They're comfortable and you get to see a lot of the countryside.

Q: Have you read the results of Travel Today's annual survey? It seems like a lot of people

have
~~has~~ decided to take vacations closer to

chosen
home. And many people have ~~choose~~ not to go away at all this summer.

just booked
A: Not me! I've ~~booked just~~ a vacation to Australia.

been
I've never ~~was~~ to that part of the world, and I can't wait to go!

EXERCISE 6

Answers will vary.

EXERCISE 1

2. become
3. begun
4. buy
5. decided, decided
6. felt
7. get, got
8. gave, given
9. went, gone
10. had
11. live, lived
12. make
13. met, met
14. moved, moved
15. paid, paid
16. read, read
17. risen
18. see, saw
19. started, started
20. take, took

EXERCISE 2

3. Tom has gone OR has been
4. Tom got
5. Tom has made
6. Tom met
7. Tom has been
8. Tom looked
9. Tom bought
10. Tom has paid
11. Tom has read
12. Tom has managed
13. Tom has given
14. Tom felt

EXERCISE 3

2. got
3. 've been
4. did . . . have
5. became
6. had
7. were
8. did . . . last
9. divorced
10. Did . . . have
11. didn't
12. 've managed
13. saw
14. have become
15. Has . . . remarried
16. hasn't
17. did . . . fail
18. got
19. didn't know
20. did . . . meet
21. were
22. did . . . move
23. 've lived

EXERCISE 4

2. began
3. got
4. had
5. was
6. has risen
7. occurred
8. has created
9. started
10. had
11. were
12. has . . . increased
13. stayed
14. got
15. has changed
16. has reached

EXERCISE 5

Last month, I ~~have met~~ *met* the most wonderful guy. His name is Roger, and he's a student in my night class.

He ~~lived~~ *'s lived* here since 2007. Before that he lived in Detroit too, so we have a lot in common. Roger ~~has been~~ *was* married for five years but got divorced last April.

Roger and I ~~managed~~ *have managed* to spend a lot of time together in spite of our busy schedules. Last week I saw him every night, and this week ~~we~~ *we've* already gotten together three times after class. I find that I miss him when we're apart!

Monday night we ~~have seen~~ *saw* a great movie. ~~Did you see~~ *Have you seen* The Purple Room? It's playing at all the theaters.

We've decided to take a trip back to Detroit in the summer. Maybe we can get together. It would be great to see you again. Please let me know if you'll be there.

P.S. Here's a photo of Roger that ~~I've taken~~ *I took* a few weeks ago.

EXERCISE 6

Answers will vary.

EXERCISE 1

2. She's been writing articles about global warming since last month OR for a month.
3. Amanda and Pete haven't been living in New York since a few years ago OR for a few years.
4. They've been living in Toronto since 2009 OR for _____ years.
5. They've been driving a fuel-efficient car since last year OR for a year.
6. Pete hasn't been working since last year OR for a year.
7. Pete and Amanda have been thinking of traveling to Africa since last year OR for a year.
8. Amanda has been reading a lot about Africa for a few months OR since a few months ago.
9. Pete has been studying zoology since last month OR for a month OR since he went back to school (last month).
10. Amanda and Pete have been looking for a new apartment since a month ago OR for a month.

EXERCISE 2

2. has written
3. has won
4. has been
5. has received
6. has been working
7. has been teaching
8. has been taking
9. has stopped
10. has . . . been organizing
11. has designed
12. (has) developed
13. have been watching
14. has not been teaching
15. has not stopped
16. has been traveling
17. (has been) giving
18. has gone

EXERCISE 3

2. They've been eating meat-free meals one day a week.
3. They've been using pesticides.
4. They've been choosing OR They've chosen energy-efficient appliances.
5. They've been reducing OR They've reduced home heating and electricity use.
6. They haven't been recycling paper, cans, and bottles.
7. They've bought a fuel-efficient car.
8. They haven't been walking, biking, car pooling, or taking public transportation.
9. They haven't chosen a home close to work or school.
10. They haven't taken a vacation close to home.

EXERCISE 4

2. Has he won any awards?
   Yes. He's won many awards.
3. How long has he been retired?
   He's been retired since 2001 (OR for _____ years).
4. How many honorary degrees has he received?
   He's received more than 20.
5. How long has his foundation existed?
   It's existed since 1990 (OR for _____ years).
6. What has the Foundation been teaching young people?
   It's been teaching them about the importance of a healthy environment.
7. What activity has Suzuki stopped?
   He's stopped going on vacations that require air travel.
8. Has he developed a lot of TV shows?
   Yes. He's developed many TV shows.
9. How long have people been watching *The Nature of Things*?
   They've been watching it for over 30 years.
10. What has Suzuki been doing to spread his message?
    He's been traveling and giving speeches.

EXERCISE 5

It's the second week of the fall semester. I've
been taking
~~taken~~ a course on environmental issues with
Professor McCarthy. He's an expert on the subject of
                              written
global warming, and he's already ~~been writing~~ two
books on the topic. I think one of them has even
won
~~been winning~~ an award.
                                   been
    For the past two weeks, we've studying pollution
                   ^
                 has
and how the Earth's temperature ~~have~~ been getting
warmer. As part of the course, we've been reading
a lot of books on the environment. For example,

                 finished
I've just ~~been finishing~~ a book called *The Sacred
Balance: Rediscovering Our Place in Nature* by David
Suzuki. He's a well-known Canadian scientist and
environmentalist. It was fascinating. Since then,
          been reading
I've also ~~read~~ his autobiography. I've only
  read
~~been reading~~ about 50 pages of the book so far, but it
seems interesting too. I'm really learning a lot in this
course, and I've ~~been~~ started to change some of the
things I do in order to help protect the planet.

EXERCISE 6

Answers will vary.

UNIT 13 (pages 77–85)

EXERCISE 1

3. can read an English newspaper . . . could (read one)
4. couldn't read an English novel . . . can't (read one)
5. can speak on the phone . . . couldn't (speak on the phone)
6. couldn't speak with a group of people . . . can (speak with a group of people)
7. could write an email . . . can (write one)
8. Before the course, he couldn't write a business letter, and he still can't (write one).
9. Now he can order a meal in English, and he could (order a meal in English) before too.
10. Now he can go shopping, and he could (go shopping) before too.

SUMMARY: can . . . could

EXERCISE 2

2. A: What languages can you speak?
3. A: Could you speak Spanish when you were a child?
   B: No, I couldn't.
4. A: Could you speak French?
   B: Yes, I could.
5. A: Before you came here, could you understand spoken English?
   B: No, I couldn't.
6. A: Can you understand song lyrics?
   B: Yes, I can.
7. A: Before this course, could you write a business letter in English?
   B: No, I couldn't.
8. A: Could you drive a car before you came here?
   B: No, I couldn't.
9. A: Can you drive a car now?
   B: No, I can't.

10. **A:** Can you swim?
   B: Yes, I can.
11. **A:** Could you surf before you came here?
   B: No, I couldn't.
12. **A:** What can you do now that you couldn't do before?
   B: can do . . . couldn't do

EXERCISE 3

2. can damage	**7.** can . . . do
3. can recover	**8.** can understand
4. can't survive	**9.** can't leave
5. can lose	**10.** can't be
6. can listen	

EXERCISE 4

2. are able to interpret
3. are not able to distinguish
4. are not able to understand
5. are able to hear
6. are able to get back
7. are able to read
8. is not able to recognize
9. is not able to work
10. are able to communicate

EXERCISE 5

3. How will . . . be able to see
4. Will . . . be able to hear
5. No, you won't.
6. How will . . . be able to solve
7. Will . . . be able to enjoy
8. Yes, you will.

EXERCISE 6

2. could read	**9.** can speak
3. couldn't accept	**10.** was able to achieve
4. was able to accept	**11.** will be able to get
5. could see	**12.** can read
6. will . . . be able to do	**13.** can change
7. can do	**14.** can do
8. can do	

EXERCISE 7

Before I came to this country, I ~~can't~~ *couldn't* do many things in English. For example, I couldn't follow a conversation if many people were talking at the same time. I always got confused. I remember a party I went to. Everyone was speaking English, and I wasn't able *to* understand a word! I felt so

uncomfortable. Finally, my aunt came to pick me up, and I ~~could~~ *was able to* leave the party.

Today I can ~~to~~ understand much better. I am taking classes at the adult center. My teacher is very good. She can ~~explains~~ *explain* things well, and she always gives us the chance to talk a lot in class. When I finish this class in May, I ~~can~~ *will be able to* speak and understand a lot better.

Speaking English well is very important to me. I practice a lot at home too. When I first came to this country, I ~~can't~~ *couldn't* OR *wasn't able to* understand very much TV, but now I can ~~to~~ understand much better. In fact, I can do a lot now, and I think in a few more months I ~~can~~ *'ll be able to* do even more.

EXERCISE 8

Answers will vary.

UNIT 14 (pages 86–89)

EXERCISE 1

2. c	**6.** a
3. b	**7.** e
4. h	**8.** g
5. f	

EXERCISE 2

2. we (please) review Unit 6? OR we review Unit 6, please?
3. I (please) borrow your pen? OR I borrow your pen, please?
4. I look at your (class) notes?
5. I come late to the next class?
6. my roommate (please) come to the next class with me? OR my roommate come to the next class with me, please?
7. I (please) ask a question? OR I ask a question, please?
8. we (please) use a dictionary? OR we use a dictionary, please?
9. we (please) leave five minutes early? OR we leave five minutes early, please?
10. my sister goes on the class trip with the rest of the class?

EXERCISE 3

2. can bring	**7.** may not pay
3. can bring	**8.** may not purchase
4. can't OR cannot drink	**9.** can't OR cannot get
5. can pay	**10.** may swim
6. can pay	

EXERCISE 4

I've been sick for the past two days. That's why I missed the last test. I'm really annoyed. I studied a lot for it and was really well prepared. May I ~~taking~~ _take_ a make-up exam?

I know you never miss class, Tim, so I assumed that's what happened. I hope you're feeling better. Yes, you can take a make-up exam if you bring a doctor's note.

If I can take the exam, may I use my calculator during the test?

No, you ~~mayn't~~ _may not_! It's against the guidelines we established at the beginning of the semester. Remember?

Could my roommate ~~comes~~ _come_ to class and take notes for me on Thursday?

Yes, he ~~could~~ _can_. I hope you can read his handwriting!

Do you mind ~~when~~ _if_ he records Allison's presentation for me? I don't want to miss it.

Not at all. It's fine for him to record the presentation.

One last thing—I know I missed some handouts. May I ~~have please~~ _please have_ copies of them?

Sure. I'll give them to your roommate on Thursday.

Thanks a lot.

EXERCISE 5

Answers will vary.

UNIT 15 (pages 90–94)

EXERCISE 1

2. a	**7.** b
3. h	**8.** i
4. g	**9.** f
5. j	**10.** e
6. c	

"Yes" responses: a, b, c, e, f, g, j
"No" responses: d, h, i
Negative = "OK": j

EXERCISE 2

2. opening the window
3. buy some stamps
4. pick up a sandwich
5. staying late tonight
6. keep the noise down

7. come to my office
8. get Frank's phone number
9. explaining this note to me
10. lend me $5.00

EXERCISE 3

2. Would you mind working on Saturday?
3. Will you please help me? OR Will you help me, please?
4. Would you please text me your decision? OR Would you text me your decision, please?
5. Could you please drive me home? OR Could you drive me home, please?

EXERCISE 4

(Note 3) Will you return please the stapler? → Will you please return the stapler? OR Will you return the stapler, please?

(Note 5) Would you mind deliver → Would you mind delivering

(Note 6) Could you please remember to lock the door. → Could you please remember to lock the door?

(Note 7) Would you please to call Ms. Rivera before the end of the day? → Would you please call Ms. Rivera before the end of the day? OR Would you call Ms. Rivera before the end of the day, please?

(Note 8) Also, would you mind to email Lisa Barker a copy? → Also, would you mind emailing Lisa Barker a copy?

EXERCISE 5

Answers will vary.

UNIT 16 (pages 95–100)

EXERCISE 1

2. You shouldn't shout into the phone.
3. You should speak in a quiet, normal voice.
4. You should leave the room to make a phone call.
5. You shouldn't discuss private issues in public places.
6. You shouldn't stand too close to other people when you are talking on the phone.
7. You should pay attention to other people on the street when you are walking and talking.
8. You shouldn't use a cell phone while you are driving. OR You should never use a cell phone while you are driving.

EXERCISE 2

2. should call
3. 'd better not forget
4. a. ought to see
   b. 'd better buy
   c. should get
5. should try
6. a. ought to think
   b. should look into

7. a. shouldn't talk
   b. should be
8. 'd better not call
9. ought to have
10. should get
11. ought to have
12. shouldn't talk
13. 'd better hang up

EXERCISE 3

3. What should I wear?
4. Should I bring a gift?
5. No, you shouldn't.
6. Should I bring something to eat or drink?
7. You should bring something to drink.
8. When should I respond?
9. You should respond by May 15.
10. Should I call Aunt Rosa?
11. No, you shouldn't.
12. Who should I call?
13. You should call Amy (and leave a message at 555-3234).

EXERCISE 4

Party Etiquette Quiz

1. You're at a party and you can't remember
   someone's name. What ~~you should~~ do? *(should you)*
   a. You should ~~no~~ ask the person's name. *(not)*
   b. ~~You better~~ avoid the person or leave
      immediately! *(You'd better)*
   c. You ought ᵗᵒ just ask.

2. You don't know anyone at the party, and your
   host doesn't introduce you to the other guests.
   ~~Had you better~~ introduce yourself? *(Should you)*
   a. Yes, you should. You should say, "Hi. My
      name's _____."
   b. No, you ~~should~~. You'd better tell the host to
      introduce you. *(shouldn't)*

3. Your cell phone rings during the party.
   ~~You should~~ answer it? *(Should you)*
   a. Just let it ring. You ~~had not better~~ answer it. *('d better not)*
   b. You should answer it, but just have a short
      conversation.
   c. You really ought to leave the room and speak
      to the person in private.

4. You had a very nice time at the party. How
   ~~you should~~ thank your host? *(should you)*
   a. You should just say "thank you" when you
      leave.
   b. You should send a "thank-you" email the next
      day.
   c. You ~~oughta~~ write a long "thank-you" letter
      and send a gift too. *(ought to)*

5. Everyone brought gifts to the party. You
   didn't.
   a. You'd better ⋈ apologize right away.
   b. You shouldn't say anything, but you ought to
      send a gift later.
   c. You should leave immediately and go buy a
      gift.

EXERCISE 5

Answers will vary.

UNIT 17 (pages 101–105)

EXERCISE 1

A

Tut's Tomb: An Egyptian Time Capsule

Tutankhamun, better known as King Tut, became king of ancient Egypt when he was only nine years old. He died before his nineteenth birthday around 1323 B.C.E., and was mostly forgotten. Thousands of years later, British archeologist Howard Carter searched for his tomb. In 1922, after searching for many years, he finally found it near the Nile River, across from the modern Egyptian city of Luxor. Inside he discovered thousands of items buried along with the young king. Among the many treasures were:

- furniture—including couches and chairs
- jewelry—including bracelets and necklaces
- clothing—including gloves, scarves, and shoes
- musical instruments
- chariots
- vases and jars
- pots made of clay (they probably once contained money)
- games and toys (Tut played with them as a child)
- food and wine
- gold

Tut's tomb is a time capsule. It gives us a picture of how Egyptian kings lived more than 3000 years ago, how they died, and what they expected to need in their lives after death.

Since his discovery, Tut has not been resting in peace. He and his treasures have traveled to exhibitions around the world, where millions of visitors have been able to view some of the wonders of his ancient civilization.

B

Proper nouns: Tutankhamun, King, Egypt, Howard Carter, Nile, Luxor

Common count nouns: *Answers will vary.*
Some possibilities: time capsule, years, birthday, archeologist, river, city, items, king, treasures, couches, chairs, bracelets, necklaces, gloves, scarves, shoes, instruments, chariots, vases, jars, pots, games, toys, child, picture, lives, discovery, exhibitions, world, visitors, wonders, civilization

Common non-count nouns: jewelry, clothing, clay, money, food, wine, gold, death, peace

EXERCISE 2

2. country lies
3. people live
4. Cairo has
5. Cotton is
6. Rice grows
7. tourists visit
8. Ramadan takes place
9. shops and restaurants close
10. weather is
11. clothing is
12. sunhats are OR a sunhat is

EXERCISE 3

2. many
3. several
4. a few
5. many
6. a lot of
7. much
8. many
9. much
10. some
11. a lot of
12. a few
13. some
14. a lot of
15. some
16. some
17. some
18. many
19. Many
20. many
21. a lot of

EXERCISE 4

I can't tell you how much we enjoyed our trip
to ~~egypt~~ *Egypt*. We just returned ~~few~~ *a few* days ago. What an
amazing country! There are so ~~much~~ *many* things to see
and do. My only complaint ~~are~~ *is* that we didn't have
enough time! But, we'll be back!
Hannes Koch, Germany

We saw a lot of tombs and pyramids on our recent trip, but the best were the three Giza
pyramids. ~~It is~~ *They are* huge! And, I was surprised to learn, they are located right at the edge of the city of Cairo. Because of this, there is a lot of traffic getting there
(and back). There were also a lot *of* tourists. The day we were there it was very hot. If you go, you should
know that there are ~~a few~~ *few* places to get anything to
drink, so I REALLY recommend that you bring ~~any~~ *some* water with you. Oh, and if you want to see the inside of a pyramid, you need a special ticket, and they only
sell a ~~little~~ *few* tickets each day. Get there early if you want one!
Vilma Ortiz, USA

The food ~~are~~ *is* great in Egypt! We went to some
wonderful ~~Restaurants~~ *restaurants*. We found out about one
place near our hotel that doesn't have ~~much~~ *many* tourists.
Mostly local people ~~eats~~ *eat* there and everyone was really friendly. I particularly enjoyed the "meze" (a
variety of appetizers). You choose a ~~little~~ *few* different plates before you order your main dish. Delicious!
Jim Cook, England

There are many beautiful ~~beach~~ *beaches* in Alexandria. A lot of them are private or connected to hotels, but there are also public ones, so be sure to bring a bathing suit if you visit that part of Egypt. The water
~~were~~ *was* warm—like being in a bathtub!
Aki Kato, Japan

EXERCISE 5

Answers will vary.

UNIT 18 (pages 106–110)

EXERCISE 1

1. the, the
2. the
3. the
4. the, the
5. a, The, the
6. the
7. Ø, Ø, the, Ø
8. the, an, the
9. an, a
10. Ø, Ø
11. some, a, the, the
12. the, a, The

EXERCISE 2

2. a	13. The
3. the	14. the
4. A	15. the
5. a	16. the
6. —	17. the
7. —	18. the
8. a	19. an
9. —	20. —
10. The	21. a
11. —	22. —
12. a	23. the

EXERCISE 3

2. a	15. an
3. a	16. the
4. the	17. the
5. the	18. The
6. the	19. a
7. the	20. the
8. the	21. the
9. the	22. the
10. The	23. The
11. the	24. the
12. a	25. the
13. the	26. —
14. the	27. the

EXERCISE 4

       A fox is ~~the~~ *a* member of the dog family. It looks like ~~the~~ *a* small, thin dog with ~~an~~ *a* bushy tail, a long nose, and pointed ears. You can find ~~the~~ foxes in most parts of ~~a~~ *the* world. ~~Animal~~ *The animal* moves very fast, and it is ~~the~~ *a* very good hunter. It eats mostly mice, but it also eats ~~the~~ birds, insects, rabbits, and fruit.

       Unfortunately, ~~x~~ people hunt foxes for their beautiful fur. They also hunt them for another reason. The fox is ~~a~~ *an* intelligent, clever animal, and this makes it hard to catch. As a result, ~~the~~ hunters find it exciting to try to catch one. It is also because of its cleverness that a fox often appears in fables, such as ~~a~~ *the* fable we just read in class.

EXERCISE 5

Answers will vary.

EXERCISE 1

2. nice	11. sudden
3. fast	12. peacefully
4. well	13. angrily
5. dangerous	14. convenient
6. beautifully	15. badly
7. hard	16. thoughtful
8. safely	17. hungry
9. ideal	18. extremely
10. happy	

EXERCISE 2

2. Good news travels fast
3. It has five large rooms
4. it's in a very large building
5. it's very sunny
6. We're really satisfied with it
7. It's not too bad
8. It seems pretty quiet
9. he speaks very loudly
10. He doesn't hear well
11. Was it a hard decision
12. we had to decide quickly
13. I have to leave now
14. Good luck with your new apartment

EXERCISE 3

2. hard	16. empty
3. really	17. good
4. well	18. easily
5. nice	19. near
6. extremely	20. frequently
7. comfortable	21. nice
8. cold	22. convenient
9. pretty	23. wonderful
10. friendly	24. completely
11. safe	25. new
12. really	26. really
13. important	27. happy
14. late	28. happy
15. completely	

EXERCISE 4

2. disturbed	11. touching
3. entertaining	12. astonishing
4. disgusted	13. frightening
5. inspiring	14. bored
6. paralyzed	15. disappointed
7. moving	16. touching
8. moved	17. exciting
9. frightening	18. entertaining
10. disturbed	19. bored

EXERCISE 5

2. tall handsome Italian actor
3. large new TV
4. delicious fresh mushroom pizza
5. comfortable black leather sofa
6. nice small student apartment
7. quiet residential neighborhood
8. enjoyable, relaxing evening
9. small comfortable, affordable apartment OR
small affordable, comfortable apartment

EXERCISE 6

Charming
~~Charmingly~~, one-bedroom apartment in a
peaceful residential
~~residential peaceful~~ neighborhood.
Conveniently
~~Convenient~~ located near shopping, transportation,
entertainment, and more.
- affordable rent
- all-new appliances
  beautiful antique French
- ~~French antique beautiful~~ desk
- friendly neighbors
  safe
- clean and ~~safely~~ neighborhood
  close
- ~~closely~~ to park
- quiet building

This great apartment is ideal for students, and
immediately
it's ~~immediate~~ available. Call 444–HOME for an
disappointed
appointment. You won't be ~~disappointing~~! But act
fast   amazing apartment
~~fastly~~! This ~~apartment amazing~~ won't last long.

EXERCISE 7

Answers will vary.

UNIT 20 (pages 117–123)

EXERCISE 1

2. worse
3. bigger
4. more careful
5. cheaper
6. more comfortable
7. more crowded
8. more delicious
9. earlier
10. more expensive
11. farther OR further
12. fresher
13. better
14. hotter
15. noisier
16. more relaxed
17. more terrible
18. more traditional
19. more varied
20. wetter

EXERCISE 2

2. not as large as
3. just as big as
4. just as expensive as
5. not as varied as
6. not as long as
7. not as convenient as
8. not as late as
9. not as nice as
10. just as good as
11. not as good as
12. just as clean as

EXERCISE 3

2. earlier
3. more comfortable
4. healthier than
5. more interesting than, better than, fresher
6. taller than
7. worse, quieter (OR more quiet) than, more relaxed
8. later than
9. faster
10. easier

EXERCISE 4

2. Y . . . cheaper than . . . X
3. Y . . . larger than . . . X
4. X . . . smaller than . . . Y
5. Y . . . heavier than . . . X
6. X . . . lighter than . . . Y
7. X . . . more efficient than . . . Y
8. Y . . . more effective than . . . X
9. Y . . . faster than . . . X
10. X . . . slower than . . . Y
11. X . . . noisier than . . . Y
12. Y . . . quieter (OR more quiet) than . . . X
13. Y . . . better than . . . X
14. X . . . worse than . . . Y

EXERCISE 5

2. cheaper and cheaper OR less and less expensive
3. better and better
4. bigger and bigger
5. more and more varied
6. more and more popular
7. less and less healthy
8. heavier and heavier

EXERCISE 6

2. The fresher the ingredients, the better the food.
3. The more popular the restaurant, the longer the lines.
4. The more enjoyable the meal, the more satisfied the customers.
5. The bigger the selection, the happier the customers.

6. The later in the day, the more tired the servers (get).
7. The more crowded the restaurant, the slower the service.
8. The better the service, the higher the tip.

EXERCISE 7

I just got home from the Pizza Palace. Wow! The pizza there just keeps getting ~~good~~ *better* and better. And, of course, the better the food, the ~~more long~~ *longer* the lines, and the ~~crowdeder~~ *more crowded* the restaurant! But I don't really mind. It's totally worth it. Tonight Ana and I shared a pizza with spinach, mushrooms, and ~~fresher~~ *fresh* tomatoes. It was much more interesting ~~as~~ *than* a traditional pizza with just tomato sauce and cheese. It's also healthier ~~than~~. And the ingredients were as fresh ~~than~~ *as* you can find anywhere in the city. (Although I usually think the pizza at Joe's Pizzeria is fresher.) It was so large that we couldn't finish it, so I brought the rest home. Actually, I'm getting hungry again just thinking about it. I think I'll pop a slice into the microwave and warm it up. It will probably taste almost as ~~better~~ *good* as it tasted at the Pizza Palace!

EXERCISE 8

Answers will vary.

UNIT 21 (pages 124–129)

EXERCISE 1

2. the worst
3. the biggest
4. the cutest
5. the most dynamic
6. the most expensive
7. the farthest OR the furthest
8. the funniest
9. the best
10. the happiest OR the most happy
11. the hottest
12. the most important
13. the most intelligent
14. the most interesting
15. the lowest
16. the nicest
17. the noisiest OR the most noisy
18. the most practical
19. the warmest
20. the most wonderful

EXERCISE 2

2. Mexico City . . . the newest
3. New York City . . . the longest
4. Toronto . . . the shortest
5. The busiest . . . New York City
6. Toronto . . . the lowest
7. Toronto . . . the most expensive (OR Mexico City . . . the least expensive)
8. the cheapest . . . Mexico City

EXERCISE 3

2. the newest
3. the most beautiful
4. the easiest
5. the biggest
6. the least comfortable
7. the fastest
8. the coolest
9. the hottest
10. the most convenient
11. the most interesting
12. the least dangerous
13. the most historic
14. the most crowded
15. The most efficient
16. the most dangerous
17. the least expensive
18. the quietest OR the most quiet

EXERCISE 4

Greetings from Mexico City! With its mixture of the old and the new, this is one of the ~~interestingest~~ *most interesting* cities I've ever visited. The people are among the ~~friendlier~~ *friendliest* OR *most friendly* in the world, and they have been very patient with my attempts to speak their language. Spanish is definitely one of ~~a~~ *the* most beautiful languages, and I really want to take lessons when I get home. This has been the ~~most hot~~ *hottest* summer in years, and I'm looking forward to going to the beach next week. The air pollution is also the ~~baddest~~ *worst* I've experienced, so I'll be glad to be out of the city. By the way, we definitely did not need to rent a car. The ~~most fast~~ *fastest* and ~~convenientest~~ *most convenient* way to get around is by subway.

EXERCISE 5

Answers will vary.

UNIT 22 (pages 130–135)

EXERCISE 1

2. worse — the worst
3. more beautifully — the most beautifully
4. more carefully — the most carefully
5. more consistently — the most consistently
6. more dangerously — the most dangerously
7. earlier — the earliest
8. more effectively — the most effectively
9. farther OR further — the farthest OR the furthest
10. faster — the fastest

11. more frequently   the most frequently
12. harder   the hardest
13. more intensely   the most intensely
14. less   the least
15. longer   the longest
16. more   the most
17. more quickly   the most quickly
18. more slowly   the most slowly
19. sooner   the soonest
20. better   the best

EXERCISE 2

2. ran as fast as
3. jumped as high as
4. didn't jump as high as
5. didn't throw the discus as far as
6. threw the discus as far as
7. didn't do as well as
8. didn't compete as successfully as

EXERCISE 3

2. harder than
3. more slowly than OR slower than
4. faster
5. more consistently
6. more aggressively than
7. worse than
8. better
9. more effectively
10. more intensely
11. (more) frequently

Winning Team: Jamil, Randy, Carlos
Losing Team: Alex, Rick, Larry, Elvin

EXERCISE 4

2. E . . . the most slowly OR the slowest, more slowly OR slower than
3. higher than . . . B
4. E . . . the highest
5. farther than . . . E
6. E . . . the farthest
7. E . . . the best
8. E . . . the worst . . . better than

EXERCISE 5

2. She's running more and more frequently.
3. He's throwing the ball farther and farther.
4. She's shooting more and more accurately.
5. He's jumping higher and higher.
6. He's running more and more slowly OR slower and slower.
7. They're skating (OR dancing) more and more gracefully. OR They're scoring higher and higher.
8. They're practicing longer and longer.
9. He's driving more and more dangerously.
10. They're feeling worse and worse.

EXERCISE 6

I just completed my run. I'm running much longer *than* ~~that~~ before.
Today I ran for 30 minutes without getting out of breath. I'm glad I decided to run ~~more slow~~ *more slowly* OR *slower*. The more slowly I run, the ~~farthest~~ *farther* I can go. I'm really seeing progress.
Because I'm enjoying it, I run more and more ~~frequent~~ *frequently*. And the more often I do it, the longer and farther I can go. I really believe that running helps me feel better more ~~quick~~ *quickly* than other forms of exercise. I'm even sleeping better than before!
I'm thinking about running in the next marathon. I may not run ~~as fast than~~ *as fast as* OR *faster than* younger runners, but I think I can run ~~long~~ *longer* and farther. We'll see!

EXERCISE 7

Answers will vary.

UNIT 23 (pages 136–141)

EXERCISE 1

2. going
3. meeting
4. Sitting
5. running
6. lifting
7. doing
8. taking
9. Exercising
10. wasting

EXERCISE 2

2. Dancing
3. lifting weights
4. walking (OR playing tennis) . . . playing tennis (OR walking)
5. swimming
6. lifting weights
7. walking (OR riding a bike) . . . riding a bike (OR walking)
8. Doing sit-ups
9. swimming
10. lifting weights (OR doing sit-ups), doing sit-ups (OR lifting weights)
11. running
12. playing tennis
13. Riding a bike
14. lifting weights

EXERCISE 3

2. dislikes doing OR doesn't enjoy doing
3. enjoys dancing
4. mind teaching
5. kept practicing
6. denied (OR denies) stepping OR didn't admit (OR doesn't admit) stepping
7. considering taking
8. regrets not beginning
9. suggests going OR suggested going
10. admits feeling OR admitted feeling
11. banned smoking OR doesn't permit smoking
12. permits smoking

EXERCISE 4

2. to having
3. in quitting
4. about passing
5. on staying, finishing
6. of staying, of getting
7. in having
8. of permitting, to smoking

EXERCISE 5

I'm in favor of ~~ban~~ *banning* smoking in all public places. I think ~~to smoke~~ *smoking* should be illegal in parks and at beaches.

I approve ~~to~~ *of* having free programs that help people quit ~~to smoke~~ *smoking*.

~~To advertise~~ *Advertising* cigarettes in newspapers and magazines is alright.

Smoking cigarettes ~~are~~ *is* a private decision, and the government should not make laws against it.

If people enjoy ~~to light~~ *lighting* up a cigarette, that is their right.

EXERCISE 6

Answers will vary.

UNIT 24 (pages 142–146)

EXERCISE 1

2. want to see
3. refuses to go
4. threatened to end
5. hesitate (OR am hesitating) to take
6. seems to be
7. attempted to create
8. intend to stay
9. needs to speak
10. will agree to go

EXERCISE 2

2. to do the dishes.
   him to do the dishes.
3. her to buy some milk.
   to buy some milk.
4. him to drive her to her aunt's.
   to drive her to her aunt's.
5. him to have dinner at her place Friday night.
   to have dinner at her place Friday night.
6. him to give her his answer tomorrow.
   to give her his answer tomorrow.
7. to cut his hair.
   her to cut his hair.
8. him to be home at 7:00.
   to get home at 8:00.
9. her to call him before she left the office.
   to call him before she left the office.
10. to see a movie Friday night.
    her to pick one out.
11. to ask his boss for a raise.
    him to do it.
12. to get some more stamps.
    to stop at the post office on the way home.

EXERCISE 3

Annie answered my letter. I didn't expect ~~hearing~~ *to hear* back from her so soon! She agrees that seeing a counselor is a good idea for John and me, but she advised ~~we~~ *us* to go to counseling separately at first. That idea never even occurred to me, but I think that it's a really excellent suggestion. I don't know if John will agree ~~going~~ *to go*, but I'm definitely going to ask him to think about it when I see him on Saturday. I attempted to introduce the topic last night, but he pretended ~~to not~~ *not to* hear me. (He's been doing that a lot lately. He seems to think if he ignores a question, I'll just forget about it!) I won't give up, though. I'm going to try to persuade ~~he~~ *him* to go. I have no idea how to find a counselor, so if he agrees to go, I may ask Annie ˄*to* recommend some in our area. Obviously, I want ~~finding~~ *to find* someone really good.
I still believe in us as a couple. Our relationship deserves to have a chance, and I'm prepared ˄*to* give it one. But I want John ~~feels~~ *to feel* the same way. Afterall, it takes more than one person to make a relationship. I really need to know that he's 100 percent committed to the relationship. I can be patient, but I can't afford ~~waiting~~ *to wait* forever.

EXERCISE 4

Answers will vary.

UNIT 25 (pages 147–152)

EXERCISE 1

2. You can use cell phones and smart phones to take pictures.
3. You can use smart phones to search online.
4. You can use smart phones to send email.
5. You can use cell phones, smart phones, and PDAs to connect to the Internet.
6. You can use smart phones and PDAs to create a "To Do" list.
7. You can use cell phones, smart phones, and PDAs to store addresses.
8. You can use smart phones to play music.
9. You can use smart phones to translate words.

EXERCISE 2

3. He uses most of his salary (in order) to pay his college tuition.
4. He really wants an MP3 player (in order) to download music from the Internet.
5. He's going to wait for a sale in order not to pay the full price.
6. A lot of people came into the store today (in order) to look at the new multipurpose devices.
7. They like talking to Ned (in order) to get information about the devices.
8. Someone bought a GPS in order not to get lost.
9. Another person bought a tiny camcorder (in order) to bring it on vacation.
10. She used her credit card in order not to pay right away.
11. Ned showed her how to use the camcorder (in order) to do a lot of things.
12. She'll use it as a camera (in order) to take videos.

EXERCISE 3

2. to have
3. to pay
4. to eat
5. to leave
6. to take
7. to find

EXERCISE 4

2. good enough for me to do
3. too late to go
4. fast enough to leave
5. too tired to stay
6. too late to call
7. clearly enough for me to understand
8. hot enough to need
9. too hot for me to drink
10. easy enough for him to program

EXERCISE 5

ANDREA (4:45 PM): Did you call Sara ~~for reminding~~ *to remind* her about dinner tomorrow night?

ME (4:50 PM): It's ~~to~~ *too* early to call now. Don't worry. I set my alarm in order ~~no~~ *not* to forget.

ANDREA (5:30 PM): Will you be home ~~enough early~~ *early enough* to help me with dinner?

ME (5:45 PM): Not sure. I have to stop at the hardware store ~~too~~ *to* buy some more paint for the kitchen.

ANDREA (6:00 PM): Don't we still have paint?

ME (6:05 PM): Yes. But I want to make sure we have enough paint to ~~finishes~~ *finish* the job. It'll be a major improvement.

ANDREA (6:10 PM): OK. Would it be too hard ~~to~~ *for* you to make another stop on the way home? I need some butter and eggs ~~for baking~~ *to bake* the cake for tomorrow night. ☺

ME (6:15 PM): No problem. See you soon. XOXOX

EXERCISE 6

Answers will vary.

UNIT 26 (pages 153–157)

EXERCISE 1

2. living
3. Flying
4. to get
5. flying
6. to get over
7. doing
8. to do
9. to live
10. to do
11. seeing
12. to visit
13. getting

EXERCISE 2

2. is tired of being
3. quit (OR stopped) drinking
4. believes in talking
5. forgot to bring
6. remember telling
7. stopped to get
8. afford to lose
9. refuses to live
10. intends to make
11. agreed to help
12. offered to drive

EXERCISE 3

3. It's useful to work together.
4. Being careful is smart.
5. Being anxious all the time isn't good.
6. It isn't dangerous to fly.
7. It's a good idea to do relaxation exercises.
8. It's wonderful to travel.

EXERCISE 4

I want ~~reporting~~ *to report* on my progress. I'm very happy that
I finally stopped ~~to procrastinate~~ *procrastinating* and decided ~~doing~~ *to do*
something about my fear of flying. It was really
getting in the way of my professional and social life.
~~To join~~ *Joining* this support group was one of the smartest
decisions I've ever made.
Last week I had a business meeting in Texas. Instead
of ~~drive~~ *driving* all day to get there, I was able to ~~getting~~ *get* on
a plane and be there in just a few hours. What a
difference!

I remember ~~to work~~ *working* on an important project once,
and I actually had to drop out because it required a
lot of flying and I just couldn't do it. I was anxious all
the time.
My fear was beginning to hurt my friendships too.
I was dating a woman I liked a lot and we were
supposed to go on a trip. I canceled at the last
minute because it required ~~to take~~ *taking* a plane.
Now I'm looking forward to ~~do~~ *doing* a lot of traveling. I
know fear of flying is a universal problem, but it
doesn't have to be mine! It's a big world out there,
and I plan on ~~enjoy~~ *enjoying* it.

EXERCISE 5

Answers will vary.

UNIT 27 (pages 158–162)

EXERCISE 1

2. himself
3. itself
4. herself
5. yourself, yourselves OR yourselves, yourself
6. themselves
7. itself
8. ourselves

EXERCISE 2

2. each other
3. herself
4. themselves
5. each other's
6. herself
7. yourselves
8. itself
9. ourselves
10. each other

EXERCISE 3

2. one another OR each other
3. itself
4. each other OR one another
5. myself
6. yourselves
7. himself
8. ourselves
9. yourself
10. themselves

EXERCISE 4

2. are criticizing each other OR one another
3. is going to help himself
4. are talking to themselves
5. are introducing themselves
6. are talking to each other
7. drove herself
8. blames OR is blaming himself
9. are enjoying each other's OR one another's
10. are thanking each other OR one another

EXERCISE 5

I really enjoyed ~~me~~ *myself* at Gina's party! Hank was
there and we talked to ~~ourselves~~ *each other* OR *one another* quite a bit. He's a
little depressed about losing his job. The job ~~himself~~ *itself*
wasn't that great, but the loss of income has really
impacted his life. He's disappointed in himself. He
thinks it's all his own fault, and he blames ~~him~~ *himself* for
the whole thing. Hank introduced ~~myself~~ *me* to several
of his friends. I spoke a lot to this one woman, Cara.
We have a lot of things in common, and after just an
hour, we felt like we had known ~~each other's~~ *each other* forever.
forever. Cara ~~himself~~ *herself* is a computer programmer, just
like me.
At first I was nervous about going to the party
alone. I sometimes feel a little uncomfortable when
I'm in a social situation by ~~oneself~~ *myself*. But this time was
different. Before I went, I kept telling myself to relax.
My roommate too kept telling ~~myself~~ *me*, "Don't be so
hard on ~~you~~ *yourself*! Just have fun!" That's what I advised

Hank to do too. Before we left the party, Hank and *each other* OR *one another* OR ∅
I promised ~~us~~ to keep in touch. I hope to see him again soon.

EXERCISE 6

Answers will vary.

UNIT 28 (pages 163–167)

EXERCISE 1

2. back	**7.** up	**12.** out	**17.** on
3. in	**8.** on	**13.** over	**18.** out
4. out	**9.** up	**14.** off	
5. out	**10.** out	**15.** over	
6. back	**11.** out	**16.** down	

EXERCISE 2

2. Pick out, help . . . out
3. look up
4. Set up, talk over
5. Write up
6. Look . . . over
7. Do . . . over
8. Hand . . . in

EXERCISE 3

2. clean it up
3. call her back
4. turn it down
5. wake him up
6. turn it down
7. hand them in
8. drop it off

EXERCISE 4

2. Point out common mistakes. OR Point common mistakes out.
3. Talk them over.
4. Pick out a new problem. OR Pick a new problem out.
5. Work it out with the class.
6. Write up the results. OR Write the results up.
7. Go on to the next unit.
8. Make up the final exam questions. OR Make the final exam questions up.
9. Hand them out.
10. Set up study groups. OR Set study groups up.
11. Help them out.
12. Call off Friday's class. OR Call Friday's class off.

EXERCISE 5

How are things going? I'm already into the second month of the spring semester, and I've got a lot of work to do. For science class, I have to write
a term paper. The professor made ~~over~~ [*up*] a list of possible topics. After looking ~~over them~~ [*them over*], I think I've picked one out. I'm going to write about chimpanzees and animal intelligence. I've already

looked [*up*] some information about them online ~~up~~. I found ~~up~~ [*out*] some very interesting facts.

Did you know that their hands look very much like their feet, and that they have fingernails and toenails? Their thumbs and big toes are "opposable." This makes it easy
for them to pick things ~~out~~ [*up*] with both their fingers and toes. Their arms are longer than their legs. This
helps ~~out them~~ [*them out*] too, because they can reach fruit growing on thin branches that would not otherwise support their weight. Adult males weigh between 90 and 115 pounds, and they are about 4 feet high when
they stand ~~out~~ [*up*].

Like humans, chimpanzees are very social. They travel in groups called "communities." Mothers bring
~~out~~ [*up*] their chimps, who stay with them until about the age of seven. Even after the chimps grow up, there is still a lot of contact with other chimpanzees.

I could go on, but I need to stop writing now so I can clean ~~out~~ [*up*] my room (it's a mess!) a little before
going to bed. It's late, and I have to get ~~early up~~ [*up early*] tomorrow morning for my 9:00 class.

Please let me know how you are. Or call me. I'm often out, but if you leave a message, I'll call
~~back you~~ [*you back*] as soon as I can. It would be great to speak to you.

EXERCISE 6

Answers will vary.

UNIT 29 (pages 168–174)

EXERCISE 1

2. must pass	**9.** must not leave
3. must not forget	**10.** must wear
4. must obey	**11.** must not talk
5. must stop	**12.** must sit
6. must not drive	**13.** must . . . drink
7. must not change	**14.** must know
8. must turn on	

EXERCISE 2

2. don't have to be	**7.** have to use
3. have to drive	**8.** have to carry
4. doesn't have to drive	**9.** don't have to have
5. have to drive	**10.** have to keep
6. have to wear	**11.** don't have to keep

EXERCISE 3

2. don't have to
3. don't have to
4. must not
5. don't have to
6. don't have to
7. must not
8. don't have to

EXERCISE 4

2. **A:** Do . . . have to stop
   B: Yes, we do.
3. **A:** have . . . had to use
4. **A:** Did . . . have to work
   B: No, I didn't.
5. **B:** 'll have to get OR 'm going to have to get
6. **B:** had to drive
7. **B:** did . . . have to pay
8. **A:** Has . . . had to pay
   B: No, he hasn't.
9. **A:** Will (OR Do) . . . have to get OR
   Am . . . going to have to get
   B: Yes, you will. OR you do. OR you are.
10. **B:** has to have
11. **A:** do . . . have to get

EXERCISE 5

2. You must stop
3. You must not drive faster than 50 miles per hour.
4. You must not turn when the light is red.
5. You must not enter.
6. You can't pass another car.
7. You must drive in the direction of the arrow.
8. You can't drive 70 miles per hour.
9. You can't turn left.
10. You don't have to move your car at 6:00 P.M.

EXERCISE 6

Sorry I haven't written before, but there are
so many things I've ~~must~~ **had to** do since we moved to
California. For one, I have to ~~taking~~ **take** a driving test.
My brother is lucky. He ~~must not~~ **doesn't have to** take one because
he got a license when he was a student here. And you
really have to drive if you live here—it's very hard
to get around without a car! So, I've been studying
the Driver Handbook, and I've found some pretty
interesting—and sometimes strange—things:

You can't smoke when a minor (that's someone
under the age of eighteen) is in the car.

You can use a cell phone, but you ~~has~~ **have** got to use
one with a hands-free device.

You must ~~no~~ **not** "dump or abandon animals on a
highway." (I can't imagine anyone doing this, can

you?) If you do, you will probably ~~must~~ **have to** pay a fine of
$1,000 or go to jail for six months, or both!

Did you ~~must~~ **have to** take a road test when you moved
to Italy?

I've got **to** go now. Let me hear from you!

EXERCISE 7

Answers will vary.

UNIT 30 (pages 175–180)

EXERCISE 1

2. is supposed to send
3. are supposed to provide
4. aren't supposed to provide
5. isn't supposed to pay for
6. is supposed to pay for
7. aren't supposed to pay for
8. is supposed to pay for
9. aren't supposed to give
10. are supposed to give
11. isn't supposed to supply
12. is supposed to pay for
13. is supposed to provide

EXERCISE 2

2. Item 2: She was supposed to write the month first. OR She wasn't supposed to write the day first.
3. Item 4: She was supposed to print (OR write) her last name. OR She wasn't supposed to print (OR write) her first name.
4. Item 5: She was supposed to print (OR write) her first name. OR She wasn't supposed to print (OR write) her last name.
5. Item 6: She was supposed to write (OR include) her zip code.
6. Item 7: She was supposed to write (OR include) her state and (her) zip code.
7. Item 8: She was supposed to sign her name. OR She wasn't supposed to print her name.
8. Item 9: She was supposed to write the date.

EXERCISE 3

1. is (OR was) supposed to land
2. are . . . supposed to get
3. Are . . . supposed to call
   Yes, we are.
4. are . . . supposed to tip
5. Is . . . supposed to be
   No, it isn't.

6. are . . . supposed to do
    're supposed to leave
7. Is . . . supposed to rain
    No, it isn't.
8. Are . . . supposed to shake

EXERCISE 4

2. a. Adam wasn't going to get married.
   b. He was going to stay single.
3. a. Erica and Adam were going to get married in June.
   b. They weren't going to get married in September.
4. a. They weren't going to have a big wedding.
   b. They were going to have a small one.
5. a. Erica's sister was going to select the flowers.
   b. Adam's assistant wasn't going to do it.
6. a. They were going to have a short ceremony. OR The ceremony was going to be short.
   b. They weren't going to have a long ceremony. OR The ceremony wasn't going to be long.
7. a. They were going to live in Boston.
   b. They weren't going to move to Amherst.
8. a. Adam wasn't going to change jobs.
   b. He was going to keep his old one.

EXERCISE 5

Here we are in beautiful Bermuda. It's sunny, 80°,
               's
and it ~~will~~ supposed to get even warmer later today. I'm so glad we decided to come here for our
               were
honeymoon. At first, we ~~was~~ going to go to London, but we decided we really needed a relaxing beach vacation instead. The hotel is very nice. We were supposed to get a standard double room, but when they found out we were on our honeymoon, they upgraded us to a suite with an ocean view. Tonight
               It's supposed
we're eating at Chez Marcel's. ~~It supposes~~ to be one of the best restaurants on the island.
        I'm supposed
Gotta go now. ~~I suppose~~ to meet Adam in a few
       He was
minutes. ~~He's~~ going to join me at the beach, but decided to play some tennis instead.
Thanks for offering to pick us up at the airport. We're
       arrive
supposed to ~~arriving~~ at 5:30 P.M., but check with the airport before to see if there are any delays. See you soon!

EXERCISE 6

Answers will vary.

UNIT 31 (pages 181–184)

EXERCISE 1

2. may go
3. could be
4. might be able to
5. might want
6. may not be
7. could go
8. might not understand
9. might not want
10. could stay
11. might be

EXERCISE 2

2. might buy
3. is going to rain
4. is going to see
5. might go
6. is going to work
7. might have
8. is going to call
9. is going to read
10. might write

EXERCISE 3

How are you? It's the Fourth of July, and it's
                  clear
raining really hard. They say it could ~~cleared~~ up
         might OR may
later. Then again, it ~~could~~ not. You never know with the weather.
Do you remember my brother, Eric? He says
      have
hi. He might ~~has~~ dinner with me on Saturday night. We may go to a new Mexican restaurant that just opened in the mall.
      am going to take OR am taking
I definitely ~~might take~~ some vacation time next month. Perhaps we could do something together. It might ~~not~~ be fun to do some traveling. What do you think? Let me know.

EXERCISE 4

Answers will vary.

UNIT 32 (pages 185–190)

EXERCISE 1

2. must not be
3. must feel
4. must not have
5. must know
6. must have
7. must not hear
8. must feel
9. must have
10. must not be
11. must speak
12. must not study
13. must have
14. must not eat
15. must be

EXERCISE 2

1. might
2. must
3. must
4. might, could
5. could, must
6. must, couldn't

EXERCISE 3

2. She must
3. They must
4. He must be
5. She might (not)
   OR may (not)
   OR could
6. It must be

7. It must be
8. They might be OR
   may be OR could be
9. She must
10. He might be OR may
    be OR could be
11. They must be

EXERCISE 4

2. Could
3. can't
4. Bob
5. Chet
6. could

7. might
8. Dave
9. could
10. couldn't
11. Allen

EXERCISE 5

Just got home. It's really cold outside. The
temperature ~~could~~ *must* be below freezing because the
walkway is all covered with ice. What a day! We went
down to the police station to look at photos. I was
amazed. They must ~~having~~ *have* hundreds of photos. They
kept showing us more and more. We kept looking,
but it was difficult to be sure. After all, we only saw
the burglar for a few seconds. They've got to have
other witnesses besides us! There were a lot of
people at the mall that day. We ~~may not~~ *can't* OR *couldn't* be the only
ones who got a look at the burglar! That's the one
thing I'm certain of! In spite of our uncertainty with
the photos, the detective was very patient. I guess he
must be used to witnesses like us. Nevertheless, it
~~have~~ *has* to be frustrating for him. I know the police ~~may~~ *must*
really want to catch this guy!

EXERCISE 6

Answers will vary.